GOD'S
EARLY HEROES

Illustrated

By Roger Adcock
Revised by Elsiebeth McDaniel
Illustrated by Gordon King

SP **SCRIPTURE PRESS PUBLICATIONS, Inc.**
Wheaton, Illinois; Fullerton, California; Ajax, Ontario, Canada

Contents

In the Beginning

Everyone wonders how all things began. Where did the sun come from? Why is there day and night? How did the world come to be? What is it all for?

Once there was no world. There were no people, no animals, no sun, no stars, and no sky or Earth. But even at this time there was God. God has always been living. He is living now, and He always will live. These three sentences are only true of God. They cannot be true of anyone else.

In the very beginning there was only the mighty God. The Bible says that God made the Earth and all living things that are on the Earth.

Before God began His work, it was very dark and the darkness was everywhere. Then God said, "Let there be light." And at once there was light, beautiful bright light. God was pleased with the light. He planned for the light to be over the Earth part of the time. He also planned for darkness to be over the Earth part of the time. God called the light "day" and the darkness "night." Nighttime and daytime made up the first day.

Then God made the sky above. He said, "Let there be a division of the waters in the sky from those under the world." And God called the sky "heaven." God said that it was good. Again there was nighttime and daytime. That was the second day God worked to make the world.

Next God divided all the water into lakes, rivers, oceans, seas, ponds, streams, and springs. Where the water had been, there was now dry land. God called the land "earth." Then He made green grass grow on the earth. God said, "Let there be grass and bushes and plants and trees and flowers." And there were bushes, grass, trees, plants, and flowers of all kinds. All this God did on the third day.

God planned for every growing thing to have seed. Then from the seeds would come more grass, flowers, and plants—apples, cherries, oranges, pineapples, and every fruit there is. What a wonderful plan God had!

On the next day God made two great lights. He made the moon to shine by night and the sun to shine by day. God made the stars, and as He put the stars in the sky, He planned for people to use them. The stars were to help people keep count of days, years, and seasons in each year. And again there was nighttime and daytime, the fourth day. God was satisfied with all that He had made.

Then God said, "Let the waters be filled with fish and other water life. Let the sky be filled with birds of every kind."

As soon as God had given the order, the rivers, oceans, lakes, and ponds had many fish in them. There were salmon, tuna, bass, trout, catfish, perch, and every kind of fish. God also made the whales, sea lions, octupuses, squids, walruses, frogs, turtles, and all the animals that live in the water. On this same day, God made every kind of bird. "Let the birds fly in the sky above the land," God said. God made everything which moves and lives either in the water or the air.

Then God looked at all He had made and blessed it. "Let your number increase," God said to the animals living in the waters and the birds

flying in the sky. And making creatures to live in the water and birds was God's work for the fifth day.

On the sixth day, God made animals to live on the Earth. He said, "Let there be every kind of animal—cattle, creeping things, and wildlife of every kind." On this day God made all animals. He made tiny mice and chipmunks, huge elephants, gorillas, and buffaloes. God made the animals different from one another. He made some animals with claws, some with horns, some with hard hoofs. He made some animals to run very fast. To each living thing God gave what was needed for the place where it was to live. And God was pleased with all He had made.

Then God said, "Something more is needed." To finish His work of making all things, God wanted to make something very special.

God said, "Let us make man." And God made a man. He wanted man to be in charge of all that He had made.

God named the man Adam. He made Adam by taking some soil from the ground and shaping it into a man's body. Then God breathed the breath of life into that body, and the man became alive. He could walk around. He could talk with God. God made both a man and a woman.

And God blessed the man and woman, Adam and Eve. "You are masters over all that I have made," God told them. "Take care of everything. I have given you all kinds of plants and growing things. Enjoy them. There are fruit trees for your food. And I have given all the grass and plants to the animals and birds for their food. You should be very happy here on the Earth I have made."

Then God looked at everything He had made. He saw the light and dark, the Earth, all animals, fish, and birds, and the man and woman. God was pleased with all He had made. Now everything was finished. The Earth and heaven had been made. God said, "All that has been made is good."

And God rested on the seventh day. That is why the seventh day in every week was a special day. That day was to be a day to honor God for all that He had made.

God created everything. And everything depends on Him. He is the wise and perfect One. There is no one else like Him.

—Genesis 1; 2:1-3

Adam and Eve Disobey

When God made the world, everything He made was perfect. And God blessed all that He had made. God also planted a beautiful garden in one part of the world. He called it the Garden of Eden. God placed the man and his wife in the garden. Adam and Eve were to have full charge of the garden. Everything in it was for them to enjoy.

In the very center of this garden God placed the Tree of Life and also the Tree of the Knowledge of Good and Bad. God spoke to Adam and Eve about the Tree of the Knowledge of Good and Bad.

God said, "You may eat any fruit in the garden, but do not eat fruit from the Tree of the Knowledge of Good and Bad. If you eat that fruit, you will have to die."

Now there was one animal in the garden that seemed to be very sneaky. That animal was the serpent. One day Satan ordered the serpent to go up to Eve and say, "Is it true that you are not to eat of the Tree of the Knowledge of Good and Bad? Did God say that?"

The serpent did as Satan told him to do. He asked Eve the question, and she quickly answered, "Yes."

"Oh, is that really so?" asked the serpent. "Why can't you eat fruit from the Tree of the Knowledge of Good and Bad?"

Then Eve told the serpent what God had said. "God says that we may eat fruit from any tree except the tree that grows in the center of the garden. That is the Tree of the Knowledge of Good and Bad. We are not to eat fruit from it. God says we shall surely die if we disobey Him and eat from that tree."

"That is a lie," said the serpent. "You will not die. God knows that when you have eaten fruit from the Tree of the Knowledge of Good and Bad, you will be as wise as He is. God does not want you to know as much as He does. You would know all that is good and all that is bad. God does not want you to know that."

Eve looked at the Tree of the Knowledge of Good and Bad. She saw that the fruit of it was

beautiful and would probably taste good. She told herself that the serpent must be right. So she went to the tree, picked some fruit, and ate it. Then she took some of the fruit and gave it to Adam. He ate the fruit too.

After Adam and Eve had eaten the fruit, they heard God's voice. They had always been glad to hear His voice before. But this time Adam and Eve did not answer. They tried to hide from God among the bushes in the garden. Now, for the first time, they were afraid of God.

God called again, "Adam, where are you? Why are you hiding from Me?"

"I am hiding," said Adam, "because I am afraid of You."

Then the Lord God said, "Adam, have you eaten fruit from the tree I told you to leave alone?"

"Yes," Adam said slowly, "but Eve was the one who picked the fruit. She gave it to me."

Then the Lord God said to Eve, "Did you eat fruit from the Tree of the Knowledge of Good and Bad? Why?"

"Well," began Eve, "the serpent played a trick on me. He told me it would be all right to eat from the tree."

Of course, God already knew what Adam and Eve had done, but He wanted them to tell Him. How sorry God was that the man and woman had disobeyed Him. Now He must punish them.

God was angry with Adam and Eve. He was angry with the serpent too. He said to the serpent, "This will be your punishment. You will be hated by people. For the rest of your life you will have to crawl along in the dust of the ground."

The Lord told Eve that when her children would be born, she would have pain. And God told Adam that because he had disobeyed by eating the fruit, he would have to work hard for food. He would have to plant seeds, care for his garden, and gather the vegetables and fruit from it. Life would not be easy as it had been in the Garden of Eden. God also told Adam and Eve that someday they would die. Then their bodies would become dust again.

But at the same time, God also promised to send a Saviour who would die for the sins of all people. And God kept His promise by sending the Lord Jesus. Hundreds of years after Adam and Eve died, the Lord Jesus was born. When He died, He died for the sins of Adam and Eve, for their children's sins too, and for the sins of all who would believe and who would trust Him to be their Saviour.

Then God told Adam and Eve that they would have to leave the beautiful Garden of Eden. He gave them clothing made from animal skins and told them to leave the garden. God placed an angel with a flaming sword at the entrance to the garden. The angel would keep out anyone who tried to get into the garden.

After Adam and Eve left the garden, a baby son was born to them. They called him Cain. Later another son was born. And they named him Abel.

Cain and Abel listened as their parents told them about God. They heard how much God loved them. They also learned that they could show their love for Him by making sacrifices to Him. The sacrifice was to be an animal. They were to kill the animal and burn it on an altar. The altar

was a pile of stones that was flat on top. The sacrifice could be put on the flat part to be burned.

When Cain grew up, he became a farmer. Abel grew up to be a shepherd who took care of sheep. Both young men worked hard at their jobs. Cain grew many vegetables and grain. And Abel took care of his sheep.

One day Abel took one of his lambs, killed it, and burned it on the altar as a sacrifice to the Lord. On that same day Cain also brought a sacrifice to God. Cain brought some of the vegetables he had grown. He burned them on his altar. Even though God had told Adam and his family to use animals for sacrifices—not vegetables, or flowers, or anything else—Cain thought he would do as he wanted.

In some way God let Abel know that He was pleased with his sacrifice. God also let Cain know that He was not pleased with his sacrifice. Instead of feeling sorry that he had done wrong, Cain became very angry. God said to Cain, "Why are you so angry? You can be happy if you will obey Me. But if you do not obey Me, watch out! You will find it easy to do wrong."

Cain did not change. He was still very angry with Abel because God had been pleased with Abel's sacrifice. On a day when the two brothers were out in the field together, Cain killed his brother Abel.

Later, while Cain was working in his fields, God spoke to him. "Where is your brother?" God asked. Cain said, "How should I know? Am I supposed to take care of him?"

Then God said, "Look, your brother's blood is on the ground. I know what you have done. For your punishment, the ground will not give you good crops anymore. People will hate you, and you will have to hide from them."

Cain said, "Oh, Lord, my punishment is too hard. You are taking my farm away from me. You say that You will no longer care for me. You say that people will hate me. I cannot stand my punishment."

Now, if Cain had said that he was sorry for his sin, things might have been different. God would have forgiven him. But Cain did not seem to be sorry about what he had done. He was only sorry about his punishment.

God listened to Cain when he complained about his punishment. And God said, "All right. I will tell people that they will have a punishment seven times worse than yours if they kill you. I will also give you a mark so that people will not try to kill you."

What was the mark given Cain? The Bible does not say, but the mark was something people could see.

So Cain left home and went off to settle in another place. He had a very hard life.

A little later, God gave Adam and Eve another boy. They named him Seth. After that, Adam and Eve lived a very long time. And during those years they had many more children. Some of them loved God and obeyed Him. One man who obeyed God was called Enoch. He was Adam and Eve's great, great, great, great grandson. The Bible says that Enoch always listened to God and tried to obey Him. Enoch was called "a friend of God."

—Genesis 4:1-25; 5:6-22; 1 Corinthians 15:3, 4

Noah and His Boat

God had made a beautiful world for His people to enjoy. But the first people, Adam and Eve, would not keep God's one rule. Because they disobeyed, God had made them leave the beautiful garden where they had lived.

After a time, Adam and Eve had two boys. But as the boys grew up, one son was not interested in obeying God. That son, Cain, became so angry one day that he killed his brother, Abel. And it seems that from then on things got worse and worse.

By the time that Adam's great, great, great, great, great grandson was born, people were very, very wicked. They did bad things. They had bad thoughts. God said, "Everything that people think, or do, or want to do is very bad. Only Noah and his family want to obey Me. I will destroy all the people who do not want to have anything to do with Me."

God said to Noah, "Look, the whole world is filled with crime. No one even wants to do right. I have decided to destroy all the bad people."

Then God gave Noah directions for building a boat. Noah was to build it even though he and his family did not live near the sea. And because Noah was a person who obeyed God, he began to build the boat right away.

God told Noah exactly how long, how wide, and how high to make the boat. The boat, or ark, was to have three decks. It was to have a door. And it was to have a window that went all the way around the boat.

God said to Noah, "Look, I am going to cover the Earth with a flood, and everyone will die. But I promise to take care of you and your wife and your sons and their wives. You will all be safe in the boat you are building."

Noah was one of God's early heroes. And he was a hero because he obeyed God exactly. Surely people must have laughed when Noah told them what he was doing. The people had never seen or heard of a flood. They could not imagine what it would be like to have water everywhere. Some of them said, "Noah, you are crazy! Why do you spend your time at such hard work? We don't even know this God that you talk about. And if He told us to do something as foolish as what you are doing, we would not do it."

In Bible times, people lived for hundreds of years. Noah was 500 years old when he and his sons started to build the boat. The four men took 120 years to finish it.

Noah did some preaching during the many years he worked at building the boat. He told the people God was going to punish them for their bad ways. He said God was going to send a flood. But the people did not believe him. They were not sorry for their wrongdoing. None of them wanted to obey God.

When the ark was built, God gave some more directions. "Noah, bring animals into the ark with you. Bring a pair of every living thing that creeps or crawls or runs or flies." God did not tell Noah to bring into the ark any fish or sea animals. They would manage very well even when water would cover the whole Earth.

Noah and his sons stored away food in the boat for all the people and animals. Then the four men, Noah and his three sons, began gathering together a male and female of each animal. God had also told Noah to bring seven pairs of some kinds of animals and of every kind of bird.

Finally the day came when God said, "One week today I will begin 40 days and nights of rain."

One day passed, two, three, four, five, and six days passed without anything happening. On the seventh day everyone in Noah's family and all the animals he had chosen went on board the boat. God Himself closed the door of the ark. And then it rained and rained!

Water came down from the sky and water came up from beneath the Earth. The rivers, the streams, the lakes, and the oceans had more water in them. They began to rise and flow over the land. Soon water covered all the land. As the water became deeper, the big boat floated on it. Higher and higher the water rose, but Noah and his family were safe in the ark.

What about the people who had not believed Noah? Those bad people climbed high hills and mountains. But the water kept rising higher and

higher. Soon the hills and the mountains were covered with water. There was no place for the people to go. So all the people in the world were drowned except Noah and his family.

God did not forget about Noah and the animals in the boat. After a long, long time—about five months—God sent a wind to blow across the waters. The wind helped dry up the water.

One day Noah knew that the boat had stopped moving. It had come to rest on top of a high mountain. As the water went down, other mountain tops stuck up out of the water. Noah waited for several months and then he took a raven and let it fly away. The raven did not come back.

Noah took a dove and let it fly away too. But the dove came back. Since a raven does not mind landing on a floating object, the raven Noah let out must have found some lumber or something else floating on the water, because it did not come back to the ark. But doves are not as as strong as ravens. They want to land on something steady like a tree or building. The dove could not find any place to land, so it flew back to the ark.

A week later Noah let the dove go again. This time she came back with an olive leaf in her beak. Noah knew that the water was almost gone. After another week, Noah sent the dove

out again. This time she did not come back.

Noah waited another month. Then he opened the door of the ark and saw that most of the water was gone. God had not told Noah to leave the ark, so Noah waited two more months. Then God said, "Everyone may leave the boat now."

What was the first thing Noah did after he walked off the ark? He worshiped God. Noah built an altar and made a sacrifice. He thanked God for keeping his family safe.

God was pleased with what Noah had done. He said, "I will never send a flood again to destroy all living things. As long as the Earth is here, there will be winter and summer, time to plant and time to gather crops, day and night, and both hot and cold weather."

God gave Noah a sign to show that He would keep His word. As Noah and his family looked at the sky, they saw a beautiful rainbow. God said, "I have put My rainbow in the sky as a sign of My promise."

God blessed Noah and his sons. He told Noah that he and his sons would be in charge of all animal life in the air, in the water, and on the land.

—*Genesis 6:1—9:17*

Abraham and God's Promise

Many years after the terrible flood at the time of Noah, God spoke to another man about obeying Him. This man, Abram, lived in the land of Ur, the country which is now called Iraq. The people of Ur worshiped the moon and sun. This was wrong! They should have prayed to the Lord God, who made the sun and moon.

God told Abram to move away. So Abram left his home, his relatives, and his friends. He took his wife along and his nephew Lot and many servants. Abram did not know where he was going, but he believed that God would take care of him.

This is the promise that God made to Abram: "Leave your own country and your people. Go to the land that I will show you. If you obey Me, I will bless you." God did not tell Abram that He would harm him if he did not obey. Abram must have obeyed because he loved God and trusted Him.

Day after day after day, Abram and his family and his many servants traveled. Perhaps they traveled at night, too, when it was cool. They had to cross a large desert—dry and dusty land with no grass or water or trees. It was hard to go on and on over this land. There were mountains to cross also. And all the time, none of the people knew exactly where they were going. But Abram knew that He was obeying God.

Finally, Abram and his family and servants reached the new land. They set up their tents. Near a place called Shechem, God came to Abram and said, "I am going to give this land to you and to your children and your children's children. It will always be in your family." And Abram built an altar and worshiped God.

God blessed Abram by giving him many cows, goats, and sheep. Abram's nephew Lot had many cattle too. But the servants of Lot began to make trouble with Abram's servants. They fought and argued about which were the best places to take the cattle for food. The men who took care of Lot's cattle tried to get the best pastures for themselves. Then Abram's servants would try to take the land from them.

One day Abram said, "Look, our men are fighting all the time. Let's divide the land and each of us take part of it. Which part do you want?" Abram kindly gave Lot first choice. Lot looked over the land to find the best part. He decided to live near the city of Sodom. And Abram kept the land where his men had been taking care of the cattle.

One day God made some special promises to Abram. God promised to give Abram a son. Abram and his wife Sarah did not have a child at that time. God said again, "I will be your God and you will be My people." Then God gave Abram a new name. "From now on," God said, "you shall be called Abraham."

The Lord came to Abraham again. It was on a hot day while Abraham was sitting in the open doorway of his tent. Three messengers came to him. Abraham jumped up and ran to meet them. He said, "Sit down here. I will get some food for you and water to wash your tired feet."

The Lord had sent these men to talk with Abraham. They said, "Do as you have said, Abraham." And Abraham went into the tent where his wife Sarah had been listening. "Hurry, Sarah," Abraham said, "take some flour and bake some bread."

Then Abraham went out to his herd of cattle and told a servant to hurry and butcher one of the calves. When the meat had been cooked, Abraham took it, the bread, and some milk and put the food before the men.

"Where is your wife?" asked one of the men. "In the tent," said Abraham. The men wanted to be sure that Sarah could hear what they were going to say. The men told Abraham that the Lord was going to give a son to him and Sarah.

The men had another message for Abraham. But it was not a happy message. "God is going to burn up the city of Sodom," they said. "The city is filled with bad people. They do not love God nor worship Him. Now He is going to do away with them."

After giving this message, the men left. Then Abraham thought of Lot. "What will happen to Lot?" Abraham must have wondered.

"Lord," said Abraham as he began to talk to God, "You are going to destroy Sodom. Will you destroy it if there are 50 good people in the city?" And God answered Abraham, "If I find 50 people who love Me, I will not hurt the city."

"But what if You only find 45?" Abraham asked. Again God said that He would leave the city alone. Abraham kept on. He changed the number each time till he got it down to 10. "Yes, even for 10," said God, "I will not hurt the city."

God knew that Abraham was trying to help Lot. That very evening God sent two angels to Lot's house in Sodom. "Come with us," they said. "God is going to destroy the city."

Early the next morning, the two angels, Lot, his wife, and his two daughters were ready to leave Sodom. "Run for your lives," said the angels. "Don't look back. Run to the mountains."

The sun was rising as Lot and his family hurried across the land to safety. As God rained down fire from heaven on Sodom, Lot's wife had to find out what was happening. She disobeyed God and looked back at the city. Then, right where she stood, God changed her into a statue made of salt. But Lot and his daughters ran on till they found a cave where they could stay.

When the time came that Abraham and his wife Sarah had the son that God promised, they named the baby Isaac. How happy they were as they watched their baby grow.

Abraham loved God and tried to obey Him. But now God had one more test for Abraham. God wanted Abraham to find out for himself just how much he loved the Lord. Would he really do anything the Lord asked him to do?

One day God said, "Abraham, take your son

Isaac, whom you love, and go to burn him as a sacrifice to Me."

Abraham felt terrible! His son! His dear son whom God had sent. Now did God want his son killed? But Abraham believed God. He loved God and wanted to obey Him. He would obey Him!

Early the next morning Abraham saddled his donkey and got some wood together for a fire. Then he called Isaac and two young men who were his servants. Abraham did not tell the others what he was going to do.

Abraham, Isaac, and the two young men started off toward the mountains. It took three days to get to the mountains.

On the third day Abraham said to the young men, "You stay here with the donkey. My boy and I will go on to make a sacrifice to God."

Then Abraham tied the wood on Isaac's back. Abraham carried a knife and a piece of flint to strike for making a fire.

"Father," said Isaac, "I see that we have the wood and the flint to make the fire, but what are you going to use for the sacrifice?"

"God will see to that," said Abraham.

When they came to the exact spot where God had told Abraham to make the sacrifice, they stopped. Abraham built an altar. He put the wood on it. Then he tied Isaac with some ropes and put him on the altar. Everything was ready. Abraham took the knife and lifted it up. Just then Abraham

17

heard the Angel of God calling to him from heaven. "Abraham! Abraham!"

Abraham waited. What now? Then the Angel of God went on to say, "Lay down your knife, Abraham. Do not hurt your boy. I see that you love God most of all. You do not have to give Him your son. Look behind you."

When he turned around, Abraham saw a ram caught in a bush. He took his son off the altar and used the ram for a sacrifice.

Then the Angel of God spoke again. He told Abraham that the Lord was going to bless him. "You have obeyed the Lord," said the Angel. "Now God will bless you in ways that you cannot even imagine. You will be a blessing to all people on the Earth. And you will be a blessing because you have obeyed God."

—Genesis 12:1-7; 13:2, 5-12; 18:1-33;
19:1, 15-26, 30; 21:1-8; 22:1-18

Joseph, Adviser to the King

saac grew up to be a fine young man. Both his mother and father loved him very much. One day Isaac married a beautiful girl from his father's hometown.

Later on, Isaac and his wife had twin boys. At last Abraham had grandsons! How proud he must have been of the twins, Jacob and Esau.

Esau had been born a few minutes before Jacob. Being the oldest son was very important in Bible days. The oldest son was given what was called the birthright. The birthright meant that when the father died, the oldest son usually got twice as much as the other sons.

Esau, who had the birthright, did not think very much of the honor when he grew up. One day he came home very hungry. He saw Jacob eating some delicious stew. "Give me some," said Esau.

Jacob looked at the bowl of stew and then at hungry Esau. "All right," said Jacob, "I will give you all the stew you want if you will trade me your birthright for it."

"Agreed," said Esau. And he took the bowl of stew and hungrily ate every bit of it.

When Isaac was a very old man, he decided to bless Esau and give him his birthright. Isaac told Esau to catch a deer and cook the meat.

Jacob heard about this. He was not going to let Esau have the birthright when he had already given it away for a bowl of stew. Jacob told his mother, and she agreed to help him. Jacob's mother made some stew—the kind Isaac liked best. Then Jacob dressed up in Esau's clothes. Esau had quite a bit of hair on his arms, hands, and neck. Since Isaac was blind, Jacob's mother decided that if she tied goatskins over Jacob's arms, Isaac would think Jacob was Esau.

Jacob brought the stew to blind Isaac. He told his father that he was Esau. Then Isaac blessed Jacob and gave him all the rights that belonged to the oldest son.

As soon as Jacob had the blessing, he went out of the room. And he left just in time, for

Esau came in with his stew.

When Esau found out what Jacob had done, he wanted to kill Jacob. Isaac had given Esau a blessing, but it had not been the special blessing that belonged to the oldest son.

Isaac was afraid that Esau would kill Jacob, so he decided to send Jacob away to an uncle's home. There Jacob stayed for many years.

One day, many years later, Jacob decided to stop working for his uncle and go back to the place where he had lived as a boy. On the way home, Jacob heard that Esau was coming to meet him. Jacob was afraid that Esau would kill him, so he asked God for help.

Finally the day came when Jacob and Esau did meet. Esau had brought 400 men with him. As Jacob walked to meet his brother, he stopped and bowed seven times. Then Esau ran to meet Jacob. He was not angry.

Jacob and his family moved to the land where Jacob had been born. As time went on, Jacob got many flocks. He was a very rich man. He had 12 sons, but Jacob loved one son, Joseph, more than all the rest.

Jacob did not mind letting his other sons and daughters know that he loved Joseph most of all. One day Jacob gave a special coat to Joseph. The coat was beautiful, much better than the clothing any of the others had.

Joseph's brothers hated him because his father loved him most of all. But there was something else that made Joseph's brothers hate him. Joseph had two dreams and told about his dreams. In his dreams Joseph's brothers had bowed down to him. Now, the ten brothers were older than Joseph, and they did not intend to bow down to him. They thought he was acting smart to even think that he was better than they. "So you want to be our king?" they asked.

From that time on Joseph's brothers wanted to get even. And one day they had their chance.

Jacob had sent the ten brothers with his flocks to find pastureland. Then, after the brothers had been gone a long time, Jacob asked Joseph to go see how they were doing.

Joseph started after his brothers. After a few days, he found them. But they had seen him first. The brothers were waiting for Joseph and had a plan to do away with him.

"Here comes the dreamer," one brother said to the others. "Come on, let's kill him. Then we'll throw his body in a well and tell our father that wild animals must have killed Joseph."

One brother, Reuben, did not agree. Reuben said, "Don't kill Joseph. Throw him into a well, but don't kill him." Reuben hoped that he could get Joseph out of the well and take him safely home.

When Joseph got to the brothers, they pulled off his coat and threw him into an empty well. Then the brothers began to eat their supper. While the others were eating, Reuben went off to look for some straying sheep.

"Look," said one of the brothers to the others, "I see some men coming along. I wonder if they would like to buy Joseph. Let's sell him. Then we won't have to kill him."

The others thought it was a good idea too. They pulled Joseph up from the well and sold him to the traders.

A little later Reuben came back. Of course, he was very upset when he saw that Joseph was gone. The other brothers did not pay any attention to him. They killed an animal and splashed its blood on Joseph's coat. Then they took the coat to their father. "Do you think this is Joseph's coat?" they asked. "We found it on our way home."

When Jacob saw the coat, he said, "That is Joseph's coat. Some wild animal has killed him. Oh, my son, my son!"

The men who had bought Joseph took him to Egypt. Then they sold Joseph to Potiphar, an officer to the king of Egypt.

Joseph worked hard in Potiphar's house. Everyone liked him. Potiphar himself noticed that Joseph loved the Lord. He saw, too, that the Lord was taking care of Joseph. Then the Lord began blessing Potiphar for being kind to Joseph. And when Joseph was on the job, Potiphar had nothing to worry about.

But one person was not happy with Joseph. That was Potiphar's wife. She wanted Joseph to be her boyfriend. Joseph knew that a married lady should not have a boyfriend. But Potiphar's wife lied about Joseph. She made Potiphar believe that Joseph was her boyfriend.

Of course, Potiphar was angry. He sent Joseph to prison. But the Lord was still with Joseph even while he was in prison. There God gave Joseph the power to explain dreams. Joseph said to one of the men whose dream he had explained, "Tell the king about me. I don't belong in Egypt. If there is any way to get back to my own country, I'd like to go home."

But the man forgot all about Joseph. Then one day, about two years later, the king had a dream. When the man saw that no one could help the king with his dream, he suddenly thought of Joseph. The king decided that Joseph might be helpful to him and sent for him.

Now, the king had dreamed that there were seven fat cows eating grass. Suddenly, seven skinny cows came along and ate the seven fat cows. Joseph listened to the dream. Then he said, "I cannot tell you about your dream by myself, but God will help me."

And God helped Joseph explain the dream. Joseph said to the king, "You are going to have seven years when there will be plenty of food for everyone. But after the seven years, there will be another seven years when there won't be enough food for everyone."

Then Joseph told the king what he ought to do. "God has shown you what is going to happen," said Joseph. "It would be a good idea for you to put someone in charge of storing grain. During the seven good years you could store enough grain to take care of everyone during the bad years."

The king listened very carefully. Then he decided that Joseph would be the best person to put in charge. From then on, Joseph was almost as powerful as the king himself.

Now, Jacob's sons had never told their father what really had happened to Joseph. No one in the family knew that Joseph was alive and living in Egypt.

When the bad years came, Joseph's brothers and their families did not have enough grain. Jacob was a very old man by now, but he was still in charge of the family. He told his sons to go down to Egypt to buy some grain.

The ten sons went to Egypt. And because Joseph was in charge of all the grain, they had to see him. The brothers did not know that the man was Joseph. Joseph knew right away that the ten men were his brothers, but he pretended that he did not know them.

"Where are you from?" Joseph asked his brothers. "I believe you have come from another country to find out whether Egypt has enough soldiers to fight you."

"Oh, no," said the brothers. "We have come to buy grain. That is all we want."

"You are spies," said Joseph.

The brothers were afraid. They wanted Joseph to believe them, so they said, "We are ten brothers. There was another brother, but he is dead. And our youngest brother is at home."

"Well," said Joseph, "I'll find out if your story is true. I will keep you in jail while one of you goes home and brings your youngest brother."

The brothers would not agree to Joseph's plan. So Joseph put all ten men in jail for three days. At the end of the three days, Joseph had the brothers brought to him. "I have changed my mind," he said. "Only one of you must stay. The rest of you may go home and bring your youngest brother."

The nine brothers started home. When they got there and told Jacob what they had to do, he said no. "Look," Jacob said, "I have already lost my dear son Joseph. You are not going to take Benjamin away too."

Then Reuben said, "Look, Father, trust me to take care of Benjamin. If anything happens to him, you may kill my two sons." But Jacob would not agree.

Day after day, Jacob, his sons, and their families ate the grain from Egypt. One day it was almost gone. Jacob called his sons to him. "Sons, you will have to go back to Egypt."

Of course the sons did not want to go. "We can't go back," one of them said. "That man in charge of the grain was not fooling. If you want us to go back, we'll have to take Benjamin."

Jacob felt terrible, but the family had to have food. "All right," he said.

When the ten brothers and Benjamin got to Joseph's palace, Joseph said, "How is your father? Is he still alive? And is this your youngest brother?" Then Joseph had to leave the room. He was ready to cry and he did not want his brothers to see how he felt.

Again Joseph sold grain to the brothers. He told a servant to hide his silver cup in Benjamin's sack of grain. Then he told his brothers good-bye, and they started on their way.

The brothers had not traveled far before one of Joseph's servants came riding after them. "Stop, thieves!" he yelled.

The servant explained that Joseph's special silver drinking cup was missing. He thought that the youngest brother had it in his sack.

"We don't have his cup," said one of the men. But the servant would not give up. Finally, Benjamin's grain sack was untied. There at the top was Joseph's special cup.

Joseph was home when the brothers came back with the servant. "What were you trying to do?"

asked Joseph. "Why did you want to steal from me? Now this young man will have to go to prison for what he has done."

The brothers knew that they could not let Benjamin go to prison. That would kill their father! One brother said, "Oh, sir, please do not send Benjamin to prison. I will gladly go in his place. If anything happens to Benjamin, my father will be so upset that he will die."

Joseph could not stand it any longer. He had been testing his brothers. Now he could see that they wanted to be kind. He told his servants to leave. Then he said, "I am Joseph."

The brothers were so surprised that they could not speak. Perhaps they thought, "If this is Joseph, he really has a chance to get even with us."

Joseph said, "I know you did wrong to me, but God took care of me. Here I am, the most important man in the land, next to the king himself. Go home now. Bring my father with you when you come back. We can all live here in Egypt and be happy together."

When the brothers got home to Jacob, they called out, "Father, Joseph is alive!"

At first Jacob could not believe the good news. But the brothers kept telling him things about Joseph until he did believe. Then Jacob moved to Egypt with all of his sons and their families. And they lived there for many years.

—*Genesis 25:21-34; 27:1—28:5; 31:17-20; 32:6, 7, 9-12; 33:1-4; 37:1-36; 39:1—46:6*

Moses, God's Chosen Leader

"See how many Israelites there are living in our land?" said the king of Egypt to one of his officers. "Once there were only a few of them, but now there are thousands of them! Soon they will be more powerful than we Egyptians are. We must do something about it!"

Long before, the Israelites had come to the land of Egypt when Joseph had brought his brothers and his father, Jacob, to live with him. And Joseph's children's children and their children's children had gone right on living in the land of Egypt. Because Jacob's second name was Israel, his people were called Israelites.

For a long time the Egyptians and the Israelites had gotten along very well together. But after hundreds of years, things changed. The new Egyptian king, or Pharaoh, did not know anything about Joseph. He was afraid of the Israelites. He thought they might become so powerful that they would take over the land.

Now Pharaoh, the king, told his people, "The Israelites are dangerous to us because there are so many of them. Let's find a way to take care of this. We will make slaves of them and give them hard work to do."

Pharaoh had been planning to build two cities where he would store all his jewels and gold. So now he gave the Israelites the hard work of building these cities. He also put cruel masters in charge of the Israelites to make them work very hard. But the more the Egyptians made the Israelites work, the stronger the Israelites seemed to be. And the Israelite women seemed to have more babies than ever before. And so there were more Israelites than ever before.

Pharaoh kept on trying to make the Israelites suffer. He made them work hard and long in the fields. Then he made other Israelites carry heavy loads of brick and mortar. But God was taking care of the Israelites. He kept them well and strong.

Pharaoh saw that he could not make the Israelites die because of working too hard. Then he thought of something else he could do. He would kill every baby boy that was born to an Israelite family. Pharaoh got his plan started by talking with the women who took care of the new babies. He told the women to kill all the boy babies as soon as they were born. But these women loved God, and they did not obey the king. They let the boy babies live. God blessed the women for doing this.

Pharaoh saw that the women were not killing the babies, so he told all of his people to kill them. He told them to watch the Israelites. "Look for baby boys," he said. "When you find a baby boy, throw him into the Nile River so that he will drown."

Now, there was an Israelite man named Amram. He and his wife had a three-year-old boy called Aaron. And they had an eleven-year-old girl named Miriam. One day a baby boy was born into their home. How much the mother and father wanted to keep him! Day after day they found a hiding place for him in their home. But one day they knew that their baby was getting too big to be kept hidden.

The mother took some grassy reeds from the river and wove them into a basket just large enough to hold her baby. She also made a cover, or lid, for the basket. She put tar, or pitch, on the outside of the basket to make it waterproof, and she lined the inside with soft cloth so that it would be comfortable. Then she put the baby in the basket and carried him down to the river.

Miriam went along with her mother to see what would happen. After the mother put the basket in the river, she told Miriam to hide in the tall grasses along the shore and watch.

Before long Pharaoh's daughter, the princess, came walking along with some of her servants. The princess saw the basket floating on the water. "Go get it," she said to one of the servants. When the servant brought the basket ashore, the princess lifted the cover, and there was the baby! He was crying, and the princess felt sorry for him. She wanted to keep him.

"Why, this baby must belong to one of the Israelites," she said. Just then Miriam, the baby's sister, came running up to the princess. She said, "Shall I go and find one of the Israelite women to take care of the baby for you?" The princess said yes, and Miriam ran off to get her mother.

When Miriam and her mother came back, the princess said, "Take this child home and take care of him for me. I will pay you well." So the baby's mother took her son home. She knew that he would be safe now because Pharaoh's own daughter had commanded her to take care of him.

Later, when the little baby had grown to be

a boy, the mother took him back to live with the princess at the palace. The princess called the boy Moses. Moses lived at the palace for many years. He went to an Egyptian school, and he learned many important things about life at the palace. But Moses never forgot that he really was the son of an Israelite, even though the princess had adopted him.

One day, many years later when Moses was a grown man, he went to visit the Israelites. He felt terrible when he saw how hard they had to work. Then he saw an Egyptian boss hit an Israelite so hard that he fell to the ground. Suddenly, Moses lost his temper. Almost without thinking he struck the Egyptian, and he hit him so hard that he killed the Egyptian. Moses looked around to see whether anyone had seen him. Then Moses hid the body in the sand.

The next day Moses was visiting the Israelites again. He saw two of the men fighting. "Stop that," Moses said.

One of the fighting men turned to Moses. He gave Moses a long look and then asked, "Remember what you did yesterday?"

When Moses knew that someone had seen him kill the Egyptian, he was afraid. And when Pharaoh heard what had happened, he ordered his men to arrest Moses. Pharaoh wanted to have Moses executed for killing the Egyptian. But before Pharaoh could even have Moses arrested, he had run off to the land of Midian.

Midian was very far from Egypt. Moses felt safe there, so he stopped to rest beside a well. As he was sitting there, seven sisters came to get water from the well. Some shepherds came to the well just as the girls got there. The shepherds chased the girls away. When Moses saw what was happening, he took the girls' side and made the shepherds give them a turn at the well.

When the girls got home, their father said, "It did not take you long to get water today."

"Father, a young man helped us," said one of the girls. "The man was dressed like an Egyptian, and he made the shepherds give us a turn at getting water."

"Well, where is he?" asked the father. "Did you just leave him at the well? Go get him. We surely want to give him supper for being so kind to you."

Moses went home with the girls and had supper. The father invited Moses to stay at their home for a time. Moses did stay there for a long time, and

he married one of the girls.

How long did Pharaoh, the king of Egypt, stay angry with Moses? The Bible does not tell. But one day Pharaoh died. Now was the time that God had planned to send Moses back to Egypt. God's plan was to have Moses help the Israelites.

One day as Moses was taking care of sheep in the land of Midian, he saw a bush on fire. Bright flames were coming from the bush, but the leaves stayed green.

"I will go see this," Moses said to himself.

As Moses came near the bush, he heard the voice of God speaking to him. "Moses! Moses!"

"Who is it?" Moses asked.

"Do not come any closer," said the voice. "Take off your shoes because you are standing on holy ground. I am God, the God of your fathers."

Moses took off his shoes. He was afraid to look at the bush, and he covered his face with his hands.

Then the Lord God told Moses why He had called him. "I have heard the Israelites crying because of the way the Egyptians have been treating them. The time has come for Me to help them. I am going to lead the Israelites out of the land of Egypt to a land that will be theirs. It will be the land that I have promised to Abraham and to the people who would be born into his family. You, Moses, are going to be the one to lead the Israelites out of Egypt."

"But I am not the one who can do a job like that," said Moses.

Then God said, "I will be with you. You tell your people, the Israelites, that it is Jehovah, the God of your ancestors Abraham, Isaac, and Jacob, who is helping them. Call together some of the older men among the Israelites. Explain what I have asked you to do. Tell them how I came to you in this burning bush. Tell them that I promise to rescue them and take them to a good land. Then you must also go to Pharaoh and tell him that I have commanded the Israelites to come here to worship Me.

"Even now I know that the Egyptian Pharaoh will not let My people go. But I will take care of him. I will cause bad things to happen. At last he will decide to let you go. And I will see that the Egyptians give you many things before you and the other Israelites leave Egypt. Don't worry. You will have plenty to bring with you from Egypt."

Moses did not know how he could possibly do what God asked. "But they won't believe me," said Moses.

Then the Lord said, "Moses, what do you have in your hand?"

"A shepherd's rod," answered Moses.

"Throw it down on the ground," the Lord told Moses. Moses threw his rod down and it became a serpent. Then the Lord told Moses to grab the serpent by the tail. When Moses did, the serpent turned into a shepherd's rod again. The Lord told Moses he could use this sign to prove that God had sent him. But Moses still said no.

But Moses said, "Please, Lord, send someone else to do the talking."

At last God said, "All right. If you don't want to speak for Me, let your brother, Aaron, do it. He is a good speaker. Your brother is on his way to find you. When you see him, tell him about the work that I am asking both of you to do. And don't forget to take your shepherd's rod along."

Then Moses told his father-in-law that he wanted to go back to Egypt. The father-in-law

"Lord, I am not a good speaker," said Moses. "I am afraid that no one will believe me."

"Who gave you your mouth?" God asked. "The One who gave you your mouth can also help you say the right words. Do as I tell you, and I will help you."

said, "Go with my blessing." So Moses started off for Egypt with his family. On the way he met his brother, Aaron. Moses told Aaron what God had asked them to do. So Moses and Aaron went back to Egypt to help the Israelites.

—*Exodus 1:1—4:20, 27-29*

Moses and Aaron Talk to the King

Pharaoh, the new king of Egypt, was sitting on his golden throne. His officers stood along the the sides of the room. Pharaoh was expecting two men, Israelites, to come to see him.

Moses and his brother, Aaron, came into the room. They carried shepherd rods with them. Aaron said, "Pharaoh, our Lord God asks that you let His people go to worship Him."

"What?" said Pharaoh. "Who is this God that He should ask to have my slaves leave their work to worship Him? The answer is no!"

But Moses and Aaron said, "God has told us that His people must go to worship Him."

"Is that so?" said Pharaoh. "Well, I will tell you something. You cannot take my slaves away. And now because you have made trouble, they will have to make bricks without using any straw to hold the clay together."

And Pharaoh gave orders that the Israelites were not to be given any straw for their bricks. The Israelites were angry with Moses because he had talked to Pharaoh. "We had an easier time before you came," they said.

Moses talked to the Lord. "Lord," he prayed, "why have you asked me to do this if Pharaoh is going to be mean to Your people?"

Then the Lord said, "Pharaoh will not give in easily. But Pharaoh, My people, and the Egyptians will see My power."

After hearing this, Moses and Aaron went back to see Pharaoh. Aaron threw down his rod, and the rod became a serpent. Then Pharaoh called on his magicians to do the same thing. Their rods became serpents, too, but Aaron's serpent swallowed their serpents! Still Pharaoh said no. He would not listen just as the Lord said he would do.

Moses and Aaron left the palace, but God told them not to give up. They were to go back the next morning. "Meet Pharaoh as he goes to wash in the river," said the Lord. "Stand there with your rod and say to Pharaoh, 'The Lord God of Israel has told me to ask you again to let His people go. You would not listen yesterday. Now the Lord has told me that He will change all the water to blood.'"

Moses and Aaron did meet Pharaoh. They said all that the Lord had told them to say. Then Aaron hit the river with his rod, and the water turned to blood. But Pharaoh would not change his mind.

The next week the Lord spoke to Moses again. "Go back to Pharaoh. Tell him to let My people go so that they can worship Me. Tell him that if he refuses to let them go, I will send thousands of frogs to swarm over all of Egypt. The frogs will be a terrible bother."

Once again the brothers went back to Pharaoh. And once again Pharaoh would not let the people go. Aaron pointed his rod toward the river, as God had told him to do, and frogs came hopping out of the river. There were frogs everywhere!

Then Pharaoh called for Moses and Aaron. "Take away the frogs," said Pharaoh, "and I will let your people go to worship their God."

"All right," said Moses, "when do you want God to take away the frogs?" Pharaoh asked that God do it the next day. And God did as He promised. The next day, the only frogs left were those in the river. But when Pharaoh saw that the frogs were gone, he changed his mind. He would not let God's people go to worship Him.

Then the Lord God told Aaron to hit the ground with his rod. "Do it," said the Lord, "and there will be lice all over Egypt." Aaron did as God said. The lice bit everyone.

Some of the men at the palace said, "Look, Pharaoh, this is God's work. Please let His people go." But Pharaoh would not.

The Lord told Moses to meet Pharaoh again. "Tell him," said God, "that if he will not let My people go, I will send swarms of flies. But in the part of the land called Goshen, where the Israelites live, there will not be any flies."

On the next day there were flies all over the land of Egypt! Pharaoh and all the people were bothered

by them. Again Pharaoh asked Moses to come to the palace. He said, "All right! You and the people worship God. But you must worship here in Egypt. I do not want you to take the people out of the country!"

Moses said, "But we do not want to do that. God has said that His people must take a three-day trip to get to the place where He wants them to worship Him."

"Oh, all right," said Pharaoh. "Get going, but do not go far. And right now, ask God to get rid of these flies. They are terrible!"

Moses promised that he would ask God to take the flies away. He also told Pharaoh that he ought to stop lying. Then Moses asked and the Lord took the flies away.

Pharaoh looked around the palace. The flies were gone! He felt good again. And he changed his mind. Quickly he sent servants to tell Moses that the people could not go.

This time God sent a terrible sickness to Egypt. The people got sick. The cows, horses, donkeys, camels, sheep, and every other animal got sick. But the animals that belonged to the Israelites did not get sick. And the Israelites themselves did not get sick. When Pharaoh heard that the Israelites and their animals were well, he was very, very angry. He said that he could never let God's people go.

But God would not give up! He told Moses and Aaron to take handfuls of ashes and toss the ashes into the air. "The ashes," said God, "will spread like fine dust over all the land of Egypt. That dust will cause boils to break out on the people and the animals."

Moses obeyed God, and every single person and animal in Egypt had boils. Boils are sores that really hurt. The king was in pain. All his officers were in pain. It was terrible! But trouble seemed to make Pharaoh more angry. It did not make him change his mind.

Then the Lord God spoke to Moses again. "Tell Pharaoh," God said, "that the Lord God says to let His people go to worship. Tell him that I could have killed him and all his people by now. I have not done this because I wanted everyone to see My power. Tell Pharaoh that I am going to send a hailstorm. Any animals left out in the storm will be killed."

Moses gave the report to Pharaoh. Then Moses pointed his hand toward the heavens and hail fell on people, animals, and plants. Thunder boomed.

Lightning flashed. Hail bounced on the ground. Never before had there been a storm like this! Everything left in the fields—men and animals—was killed. Trees were torn down. Only in the land of Goshen, where the Israelites lived, was everything all right. But Pharaoh still would not let God's people go.

God told Moses to go back to the palace. "Ask Pharaoh," said the Lord God, "how long it will be before he decides to obey Me? Tell him to let My people worship Me. Tell him that if he still will not obey, I will send locusts to the land of Egypt."

Moses did as the Lord God said. Moses said, "If you still will not let God's people go, He will send more trouble. This time He will send flying locusts to eat up anything left after the hailstorm." Then Moses walked out of the palace.

The king's officers asked, "O Pharaoh, how long will you refuse to let the people go? Don't you know that we are tired of all this trouble? We don't want any more of it."

Then Pharaoh sent for Moses and Aaron. "All right," Pharaoh told them, "go worship your God. But how many people are you taking?"

"We want to take all the people," said Moses. "We want to take our animals too."

"No!" shouted Pharaoh. "Your men can go, but you cannot take the children and animals." And Pharaoh commanded his soldiers to take Moses and Aaron out of his sight.

Outside the palace, Moses lifted up his rod as God had told him to do. Right away the wind began to blow from the east. It blew all day and night. In the morning, the wind had brought the locusts. The insects covered the land. There were so many of them flying in the air that no one could see the sun. When the locusts were finished eating, there was not one green plant left in all of Egypt.

Now Pharaoh was afraid. He sent for Moses. "Tell your God I am sorry," he said. "Tell Him to forgive my sin this one time. Then I will let His people go."

The Lord God sent another wind to blow the locusts out to sea. But again Pharaoh changed his mind. He would not let God's people go.

This time God told Moses to lift up his hand toward heaven. When Moses obeyed, God caused a terrible darkness to come over the land. It was so dark that the people were afraid to move, but in the land of Goshen it was light.

Then Pharaoh called Moses. "Let the men take their children and their wives. Go worship your

God, but leave your animals. Don't take them with you."

Moses, said, "If we go, the Lord God has said that we must take everything with us."

Then Pharaoh shouted, "Get out! I don't want to see you again ever!"

One more time God talked with Moses about sending trouble to Egypt. "I am going to do one more thing," said the Lord. "What I do will be so terrible that Pharaoh will let you go. Tell your people to be ready to march as soon as Pharaoh sends word that you can go."

Moses told all the Israelites what they had to do. "God has asked every family to fix a special meal. Choose a perfect lamb from your flock. Kill it, then take the blood from the lamb and put some of it on each side of your front door. Then put some blood above the door. Every home must have three marks of blood on it. Tonight God is going to send a mighty angel. In every home where there is no blood, the oldest son will die. But when the angel sees blood on a house, he will pass over it.

"Roast the lamb and eat it for supper. If there

is any meat left over, throw it away. And tell your family to be dressed and ready for a trip. Tonight Pharaoh will let us go. And the Lord has also told me that before we leave, we are to borrow some things from the Egyptians. When God tells us to, go to your neighbors and ask to borrow silver, gold, and some clothing. We will need all these things on our trip."

So the Israelites did as Moses told them to do. And that night, at midnight, the mighty angel took the oldest son in many homes. But he passed over every home where there was blood on the door.

Then Pharaoh and all his people were sad. Mothers and fathers cried. Pharaoh sent for Moses. "Leave us," he said. "Take your wives and children and animals. Just go!"

The Israelites were ready. They borrowed silver, gold, and clothing from their neighbors. And the Egyptians were so glad to get rid of the people that they gave them whatever they needed.

That night the Israelites started their long trip to Canaan, the land God promised to give them. God led His people. He made a special white

34

cloud to lead them during the day. At night, the cloud became fiery red so that it could be seen. Day and night the white cloud or the fiery red cloud went ahead of the people.

Now, when word reached Pharaoh that the Israelites were leaving Egypt never to come back, he was angry. He called for his soldiers and for his chariot. "We'll bring them back," he shouted.

The Egyptian army and Pharaoh rode all day. Closer and closer they came to the Israelites, who were camping beside the Red Sea.

God had already told Moses that the Egyptians were going to come after His people. And He had told Moses that the Egyptians would not be able to catch them. Moses told the people not to be afraid, but to wait and see what God would do. Then God said, "All right, Moses, tell the people to get ready to march."

When the people were standing and ready to go, God gave His next order. "Now lift up your rod, Moses," God said. "Hold it over the sea. The water will roll back, and all of you can walk across on dry ground. Then everyone in Egypt shall know that I am God."

Moses held up his rod, and the water stopped flowing. The water began to pile up to a high wall. There was a dry path across the sea. "Come on," shouted Moses, and the Israelites began walking across the sea. At that time the Lord made the cloud move around behind the long line of people. The cloud would hide the people from the Egyptians.

The Egyptian army rode up to the sea. Then the men drove their horses onto the dry path. But God gave them trouble. Their chariot wheels came off. "Let's get out of here," the soldiers said. "God must be helping those people. He is against us."

When all the Israelites were on the other side of the sea, God told Moses to hold up his rod again. Moses did, and the walls of water came splashing down on the Egyptians. The Egyptians soldiers and Pharaoh tried to ride out of the sea, but God let them drown.

When the Israelites saw what God had done for them, they really believed in Him. They were ready to do what He asked.

God took care of His people as they marched on to the land that He had promised them. In a

very wonderful way He sent manna, something like bread, to them every morning. When the people got up, the manna was on the ground, waiting for them to pick it up. This wonderful food could be eaten raw or cooked. God also led His people to wells or springs of water. He took care of their every need.

One day God told Moses to go to the top of a certain mountain. There God met Moses and gave him a stone tablet with ten rules on it. Those ten rules are called the Ten Commandments. The rules were to help God's people know how to worship Him and how to live happily together.

Moses led God's people for many, many years. During the time that Moses was leader, God told Moses to write the history of His people. Moses obeyed and wrote the first five books in the Bible: Genesis, Exodus, Leviticus, Numbers, and Deuteronomy.

When Moses was an old man, God told him it was time for a new leader to take over. Joshua, a young man who loved God, would be the one. God told Moses to place his hands on Joshua and give him a special blessing.

Then God told Moses to climb to the top of a high mountain. "You have led My people for many years," the Lord God told Moses. "From the top of the mountain you can look far off and see the land that My people will have. Now it is time for you to die and to go to be with all My people who have died." And Moses died at the top of the mountain.

When the Israelites heard that Moses had died, they were sad. "There never was anyone like Moses," they said. "Moses and the Lord used to talk together as friends. And the Lord God let Moses do many wonderful things. We shall miss our leader Moses."

—Exodus 5:1—6:13; 7:1—12:37; 13:17—14:31; 16:4-27; 17:6-13; 19:20, 25; 20; Deuteronomy 34

Balaam and His Talking Donkey

oses was dead. Joshua, the new leader, led the Israelites on their long march to the land God had promised them. God's people came to the land of Moab, where Balak was king.

When King Balak saw the Israelites coming his way, he was frightened. And all of his people were afraid, too. "Why," they said, "the Israelites will put an end to us just as cattle eat grass."

King Balak decided to send for a man who could tell what was going to happen even before it took place. The man's name was Balaam, and he lived in another country. "Come, help us," said King Balak in his message. "The Israelites are coming into our land. We are afraid that they will kill us."

King Balak wanted to know what was going to happen, but he also wanted Balaam to curse the Israelites. To curse means to ask God to let something terrible happen to the person or persons. King Balak knew Balaam was a person who talked with God.

When the messengers came to Balaam, he asked them to stay overnight. "I'll ask God to tell me what to do," Balaam told the men.

Balaam talked to God about the Israelites. He said that King Balak wanted him to curse the Israelites. God said, "Balaam, stay where you are. Do not go with these men."

The next morning Balaam told the men he would not go with them. "God has told me not to do what your king has asked," he said.

But King Balak would not take no for an answer. When the men told him what Balaam had said, he told them to go back to ask him again. "Tell Balaam," said King Balak, "I will give him whatever he wants. He shall be a great man in my kingdom."

Balaam remembered what God had said. "No, no," he said, "even if the king gives me a house filled with silver and gold, I will not do what God tells me not to do. If you will stay overnight, I'll ask God again about cursing the Israelites."

But Balaam loved money, so finally he decided to go with the men and curse the Israelites. Getting up early in the morning, he put a saddle on his donkey and started off with the men.

But God was angry. He did not want Balaam to curse His people, and He had told Balaam so.

God sent an angel to stand in the road and keep Balaam from going on.

The angel stood on the road at a place where the road went between two cliffs. The cliffs were right at the edge of the road. When the donkey saw the angel, she stopped. But Balaam beat her. The donkey tried to squeeze past the angel, but she pressed Balaam against the wall. Balaam beat her again.

The angel moved down the road. When the donkey got to him, she lay down in the road. Again Balaam beat her. Then God caused the donkey to speak. She said, "What have I done to you that you beat me three times?"

"You have made me look like a fool," yelled Balaam. "I wish I had a sword. I would kill you with it."

"Well," said the donkey, "have I ever done anything like this before?"

Then the Lord let Balaam see the angel standing in the road. Balaam was so afraid that he fell down on the ground.

"Why did you beat your donkey three times?" asked the angel. "I have come to stop you, Balaam, because you are on your way to do a bad thing. Three times your donkey saw me and stopped. If she had kept on, I would have killed you with my sword. Your donkey has saved your life."

Then Balaam said, "I have done wrong. I am doing something that I know the Lord does not want me to do."

"Well," said the angel, "I have this word for you from the Lord. He wants you to go with these men, but tell King Balak only what He tells you to say."

Balaam went on with the king's men. The king himself came to meet Balaam. How pleased King Balak was to see Balaam. The King took Balaam out to a hill. Here they could look down and see all of the Israelites. Balaam told the king to build seven altars and to prepare seven young bulls and seven young rams for a sacrifice to God.

After King Balak and Balaam had sacrificed the animals, Balaam went off by himself. He wanted to ask God what to do next. He asked, and God told him to bless the people, not curse them.

King Balak was very angry when Balaam blessed the people. He wanted Balaam to curse the Israelites. King Balak took Balaam to a different place. He built seven altars here and made seven sacrifices. Both Balaam and Balak must have thought that they could make God change His mind. But he would not. A third time the men built altars and made sacrifices. But still God would not let Balaam curse the Israelites. God told Balaam to bless the Israelites again. This was the third time.

Now King Balak was really angry. "I wanted you to curse my enemies," he said. "But you have blessed them three times. Now I am through with you. You will not get any of my silver or gold. Go on home."

And Balaam climbed back on his donkey and went home.

—Numbers 22—24

38

Joshua, a Brave Leader

The time had come for God to lead His people, the Israelites, into the land He had promised them. But to have the land for themselves, God wanted His people to take the land from the wicked people who were living there.

Were the Israelites so good that they should have the land? No, God did not say they were. But the people living in Canaan were so very wicked that God did not want them to have the good land. Then, too, many years before, God had promised the land of Canaan to Abraham and his children, some of the first Jews or Israelites.

Even though Abraham's grandson Jacob had left the land with his family, and had been living in Egypt, God was going to keep His promise. Jacob's great, great, great, great grandchildren would have the land again.

Joshua was the new leader for God's people. Moses had died and now it was Joshua's turn to lead the people. The Lord spoke to Joshua. He said, "Moses is dead. You must lead the Israelites across the Jordan River and into the land which I have promised to them. I say to you, as I said to Moses, wherever you go that place will belong to Israel. No other people will be able to fight you and win, for I will be with you. Be strong and

brave. Remember to obey Me. Tell the people to remember the rules I gave Moses."

Then Joshua gathered the people together and told them all that the Lord God had said. He also said, "Get ready to cross the Jordan River. We will start across three days from now. God will be with us if we remember to obey Him."

Then Joshua asked two soldiers to do a special job. Joshua said, "Go over to the city. See what you can find out about it. Anything you can find out about the city will help us take it."

The two soldiers obeyed and went to the city. There they came to an inn owned by a woman named Rahab. The men decided to stay there for the night. But someone had told the king of Jericho that the two soldiers were at the inn. The king sent soldiers for the men.

But Rahab knew what was happening. Even before the soldiers came, she had hidden the men in her home. She told the men to go up on the flat roof of her house. "Lie down on the roof," she said. "Take the stalks of flax that are drying up there and cover yourselves with them. Be sure you are well covered."

When the soldiers asked about the men, Rahab said, "The men were here, but they are not now.

They left the city just as it got dark and the city gates were about to close."

The soldiers hurried off. Then Rahab went up on the roof to talk with the men. She said, "I know your God is going to give our country to you. We have heard of many wonderful things that God has done for His people. Now I want you to promise me one thing. When the Israelites destroy our city, promise me that you will let me live. Also promise that you will let my mother, my father, and my brothers and sisters live, too."

"All right," said the men, "but you must get your whole family together here at your house. They will be safe here."

Rahab's house was built on top of the city wall. She took a red rope and threw one end of it out her window to the ground. One end of the rope was fastened inside her house so that the men could slide down it. Before the men left they said, "Now remember, all your family must be here in your house, and you must leave this red rope hanging from the window. Then our men will know that they are not to harm anyone here."

After the men left Rahab, they hid for a few days. Then they went back to Joshua and told him all that had happened. "The Lord will give us the whole land," the men told Joshua. "All the people are afraid of us."

Early the next morning Joshua and the people moved to the Jordan River. They camped beside the river for three days. On the third day Joshua commanded some special soldiers to go through the camp. The soldiers said, "Get ready, everyone, and when you see the priests carrying the Ark of God, follow them."

The Ark of God was very important to the Israelites. God had told Moses to make the Ark by covering a wooden box with pure gold. The inside of the box was lined with gold. On the top of the Ark were two golden angels. God told Moses the Ark would be a sign to the people that He was with them.

The people listened to the soldiers and got ready to march. The next day Joshua told the priests to take the Ark and start marching. Then the Lord said to Joshua, "Today I will show the people that I am with you as I was with Moses."

Joshua spoke to the people saying, "Soon we will cross the river, and you will see what wonderful things the Lord will do."

The priests, who were at the beginning of the long line of people, marched right into the river, and the river stopped flowing. The water began piling up till it made a wall of water. The priests stood in the middle of the river till everyone had walked across the riverbed to the other side. When everyone was safely across the river, the priests still waited. Joshua was getting his orders from the Lord, and the Lord had not told him to have the priests leave the river.

The Lord wanted His people to remember what He had done for them at the Jordan River. So He told Joshua to have 12 men put 12 stones in the middle of the river, at the place where the priests were standing. Then God told Joshua to have the men take 12 more stones and pile them on the riverside where the camp had been. The stones would remind the people of God and His great power.

As soon as the stones were in place, Joshua told the priests to come out of the river. When the priests came out of the river, carrying the Ark, the water poured down again, just as before. The people looked at the pile of stones in the river and the pile of stones on the shore. Joshua said, "Remember, when anyone asks you why these two piles of stones are here, tell them how God stopped the river so that we could cross. God did this so that all of you will worship Him forever."

The people camped out again as they waited for more orders from God. After about two weeks, God gave His orders. He said, "Jericho and its king and soldiers will soon be yours. To take Jericho, all the people are to walk about the city every day for six days. Part of the army is to go first. Then the seven priests are to be next with their trumpets. The priests carrying the Ark are to come next. Put some soldiers at the end of the line of people. Everyone in Jericho is afraid. They have heard how I brought you across the Jordan River."

Joshua listened to God's commands. He told the people what to do. "Don't make any noise," said Joshua. "The priests with trumpets may blow them, but no noise from the rest of you! Then when I say you are to shout, shout loudly!"

Everyday for six days the people marched around the city. After their march, they went back to camp. No one inside the walls of Jericho could figure out what was happening.

On the seventh day, God gave different orders. On this day the people were to march around the city seven times. As the army started around for the seventh time, the priests blew loudly on their trumpets. Then Joshua yelled, "Shout! The Lord

has given us the city!"

The people shouted as loudly as they could and suddenly the huge city wall of Jericho came tumbling to the ground. The soldiers rushed into the city. But they remembered the promise to Rahab. Joshua had told them to stay away from the house with the red rope hanging from the window.

Joshua told the two men to go to Rahab's house. "Keep your word," Joshua said. "Get Rahab and her family. Bring them here."

Then the rest of the Israelites burned the city. Everyone knew that the Lord had helped His people take the wicked city of Jericho. The wicked people who lived in the land found out how powerful God is! And they were afraid.

—Joshua 1—4; 6

42

Samson, the Strongest Man

God's people had forgotten Him! To punish His people for praying to idols, God let an enemy country capture them.

Later God sent His Angel to one of the women. The Angel came to the wife of a man named Manoah. "Soon you will have a son," the Angel said. "Be careful what you eat. Don't drink any wine or beer. And eat only food that has been prepared following the directions God has given. When your son is born, never cut his hair. He will be a special man for God. He will help God's people get their freedom."

Some months later the baby was born. Manoah and his wife named him Samson.

The Lord blessed Samson as he grew up. When Samson was a young man, he went to a nearby town. There he saw a beautiful girl. When he got home, he told his parents that he wanted to marry the girl.

"When you marry," said his father, "marry a girl of your own nationality. Don't marry a Philistine girl."

Because the Philistines were wicked enemies of God's people, Samson's father did not want his son to marry one of their girls. But Samson was very stubborn. He wanted to marry the Philistine girl. Finally his parents gave in and went with Samson to see the girl.

On the way to see the girl, a lion rushed out at Samson. But the Lord gave Samson special power and made him very strong. Samson took hold of the lion's jaws and ripped the animal apart! Somehow Samson's parents did not see this fight. Samson did not tell them about it either.

After Samson talked to the girl, she agreed to marry him. How happy Samson was as he and his parents went home.

On the way home Samson walked back to see what had happened to the lion's body. He found that some bees had swarmed into the skeleton and left a honeycomb. Samson tasted some of the honey. He gave some to his parents, but he did not tell them where he found it.

When the time came for the marriage, Samson and his parents went back to the girl's home. There, 30 young men were asked to come to the wedding supper. Samson decided to have some fun.

"Let me ask you a riddle," said Samson. "If you can find the answer, I will give each of you some new clothes. But if you cannot find out the answer in seven days, then each of you must give new clothing to me!"

The young men agreed and Samson said, "Out of the eater came forth meat, and out of the strong came forth sweetness." The Philistine men thought and thought, but they could not think of an answer. On the seventh day they went to Samson's wife and asked her help. They said, "If you don't help us, we will kill you."

Samson's wife cried as she asked Samson again and again for the answer to the riddle. "Look," said Samson, "I have not told the answer to my mother or father. Why do you think I should tell you?"

But because his wife cried and cried, Samson told her the answer. And she told the young men. Then the men said, "What is sweeter than honey? And what is stronger than a lion?"

Samson knew his wife had given away his secret. He was so very angry that he killed 30 other wicked men and gave their clothing to the 30 Philistine men who had found the answer to his riddle. Then Samson, still angry, went home.

When Samson's wife's father heard what he had done, the father was angry. "Why, Samson must hate you," the father said to his daughter. "Now he has gone home. I am going to give you to another man. Samson is not your husband."

Later Samson came back with a present for his wife. When he found out that the girl was now married to someone else, he was angrier than ever. He really would fix the Philistines!

Samson caught 300 foxes. He tied the foxes together in pairs by their tails. Then he fastened a torch between each pair. Next Samson lit the torches and let the foxes run through the fields of ripe wheat and corn. The lighted torches burned every Philistine's field. Some of the foxes ran into a grove of olive trees. The fire burned the trees to the ground.

Now the Philistines were angry. They paid Samson back by burning the girl and her father. Then to get even, Samson killed many Philistines. After doing this, Samson ran off to a cave.

Some of Samson's own people came to get him. They tied Samson with rope and led him back to the Philistines. When the Philistines saw him, they shouted for joy. But right then the Lord gave Samson His special power. Samson broke the heavy ropes as though they were thread. Then Samson picked up the jawbone from a donkey's skeleton that was lying on the ground. Because the Lord made Samson strong, he was able to kill a thousand Philistines by hitting them with the jawbone.

The Philistines must have been terribly afraid

of Samson after that. They left him alone, and for 20 years Samson was a judge over God's people.

One day Samson decided to visit a Philistine city. When some of the men heard that Samson was in their city, they closed the city gate. They hoped to keep Samson in the city and catch him. But Samson went to the city gate and lifted the two gateposts right out of the ground. He carried them to the top of a mountain. God had made Samson too strong to be caught!

After awhile Samson fell in love again. It was a Philistine woman this time too. The Philistines still wanted to catch Samson. They came to his new wife and said, "We'll give you five thousand dollars if you help us catch Samson. Find out what

makes him so strong."

Delilah, Samson's new wife, asked again and again about Samson's strength. "Why, Samson," she said, "you are so strong, I don't think anyone could catch you!"

To make her stop asking about his strength, Samson said, "If someone tied me up with new ropes, I would be very weak."

When Samson fell asleep, Delilah tied him up. Then she called to Samson, and the Philistines who were hiding nearby heard her. "Samson," she called, "the Philistines are coming to get you!" But Samson broke the ropes before the Philistines even got into the house.

Delilah tried to trick Samson again. This time

Samson said, "If you weave my hair into your weaving loom, I'll be weak."

Delilah waited till Samson was asleep. Then she wove his hair into her loom. But again when Samson woke up, he was still strong and he pulled his hair out of the loom.

Every day Delilah kept whining and asking Samson to tell her his secret. He finally gave up and told the truth. "You see, Delilah," he said, "my hair has never been cut because Gold told me not to. He wanted my long hair to be a sign that I am His special servant. If my hair is cut, I will not be strong."

Now Delilah knew Samson's secret. She quickly sent for the Philistines and told them, "We must

45

cut his hair. Then he will not be strong."

When Samson was asleep, Delilah cut his hair. Then she screamed, "Samson, the Philistines are here." This time Samson was weak. God had taken away his strength. The Philistines grabbed Samson. They put out his eyes. And they put chains around his arms and legs. Then they took blind Samson off to prison. But while Samson was in prison, his hair began to grow long again.

One day the Philistines were having a special holiday. They were worshiping the idol Dagon. From his prison cell Samson could hear their noise. "Dagon has helped us catch Samson," they yelled. Then the people screamed for Samson to be brought from prison to the temple.

Guards led Samson from prison to Dagon's temple. The guards led him to a place between two tall pillars that held up the roof. Samson asked a boy who was nearby to help him put his hands on the pillars.

As Samson touched the pillars, he prayed, "Lord, please give me back my strength just one time so that I can pay back the Philistines. I am ready to die with them if I can just do this one thing."

Then Samson pushed against the pillars with all his strength. The Lord did answer Samson's prayer, and the pillars and temple roof came crashing down on thousands of Philistines. Samson died too, but he killed more of the wicked enemies of God by his death than he had in all his life.

—*Judges 13:1-14; 14:1—15:16; 16:1-30*

Samuel, the King-maker

There was a man named Elkanah who had two wives. One was Peninnah, who had lots of children. The other wife was Hannah, who didn't have any children. Hannah wanted a child. Her husband loved her, and he used to say to her, "Am I not more to you than 10 sons?" But Hannah still wanted a child.

Poor Hannah! The other women of the town made fun of her because she didn't have any children. Their teasing bothered her more and more as the years went by. She promised the Lord that if He would give her a son, she would give him back to the Lord. Then the Lord said yes to Hannah's prayer and gave her a son, whom she called Samuel.

When Samuel was old enough, Hannah took him to another town, to Eli the high priest. Eli was pleased to have Samuel work with him in the Tabernacle. Eli had two sons who were supposed to help him, but they were bad young men who did not love the Lord. Eli was getting old. He soon depended on Samuel for everything.

One night Samuel was lying on his bed when he heard Someone call his name. Thinking that Eli wanted him, Samuel ran to him. "Here I am," he said. "What do you want?"

Eli said, "I didn't call you."

Samuel went back to bed. But he heard the voice again call, "Samuel!" He ran again to Eli, but Eli said, "I didn't call."

Then the voice called a third time, and Samuel went to Eli. He said, "You called again!"

Eli now knew that the boy must have heard the voice of the Lord. He said to Samuel, "Go and lie down. If you hear the voice again, say, 'Speak to me, Lord, for I am Your servant and I am listening.'"

When Samuel went back to bed, he heard his name once more, and this time he did as Eli had told him. Then the Lord said to Samuel, "I am going to do something which will amaze the people. I shall bring to an end the family of Eli. Eli has not bothered to correct his sons' bad ways, and they shall not be My priests. I will put you in Eli's place."

Samuel lay in bed thinking of what he had heard. The next morning he was afraid to tell Eli what the Lord had said. But Eli asked, "What did the Lord have to say to you, Samuel? Don't be afraid to tell me."

Then Samuel told him everything that the Lord had said. "It is the will of God," said Eli sadly. "Let Him do whatever is best."

—1 Samuel 1—3

The Ark of the Lord

About the time that Samuel became God's leader, the country went to war. The army was badly beaten and decided to carry the beautiful golden box, called the Ark of the Lord, with them into battle. "Then we will be sure to win," the soldiers said.

Now, part of Eli's work was to take care of the Ark of the Lord. But he let his sons take it out of the Tabernacle and off to the battle.

When Eli's sons carried the Ark onto the battlefield, everyone shouted because they thought that the Ark would bring them good luck. Now the soldiers were sure they'd win. But that was not God's plan!

The enemy seemed to grow stronger and fight harder. Not only did the enemy army win the battle, they also took the Ark of the Lord and

killed Eli's two sons.

Eli had been sitting on a bench at the roadside waiting for word of the battle. Finally, a messenger came and told Eli the awful news. How sad Eli must have felt when he heard that his two sons were dead. But when the messenger said that the Ark of the Lord had been taken by the enemy, Eli fell backwards and died. God's word had come true! Eli's family was finished!

—1 Samuel 4:1-18

Samuel as Leader

What happened to the Ark of God? Well, the Philistines who won the battle may have thought that they won because they had the Ark. They decided to take the beautiful Ark to one of their gods, a huge stone statue called Dagon. The Philistines put the Ark in front of the statue. But when they opened the temple doors the next day, the idol was flat on its face! Then the Philistines were afraid and sent the Ark back to God's people.

Now that Eli was dead, Samuel was the leader. So he called the people together and said, "You have been worshiping gods made by men. You have made sacrifices to Baal. How could you expect to win the war? If you will ask the Lord to forgive you and promise to worship only Him, He will forgive you. He will help you overcome the Philis-

tines, your enemy."

But even while Samuel was talking, the Philistines decided to come for another battle. But soon after they started marching, they stopped. A great noise seemed to come from the sky. It roared like thunder! The Philistines were afraid. They stumbled and fell. God's people chased them, and the Philistines ran as fast as they could. God gave His people the victory! And for a long, long time the Philistines did not try to fight God's people again.   —1 Samuel 7:3-17

Saul, First King of Israel

One day when Samuel was very old, some of the public officials came to him. "Samuel," they said, "you are getting very old. Your sons are not good men. They do not worship the Lord as you do. We need someone to be our leader after you are gone. Choose a king for us."

Samuel was not happy with this message. He asked the Lord what he should do. The Lord said to Samuel, "The people are wrong because they are counting on a king to help them instead of trusting Me. Let them have a king, but tell them what kind of a life they will have with a king."

Then Samuel told the people what the Lord had said. "If you have a king," he said, "you will have to work hard for him. He will ask you to make chariots and weapons of war. He will take your daughters to be cooks and servants. He will take your sons for soldiers."

The people would not listen. They said, "We will have a king! We want to be like other nations. We want a king to judge us and to fight for us."

"Give them a king," the Lord told Samuel. "Tomorrow about this time I will send you a man. Make him king over My people."

Now there was a rich man called Kish who had a son named Saul. Some donkeys Kish owned had wandered off, and he asked Saul, his son, to find them.

Finding the donkeys was hard work! Saul and his servant walked a great distance looking for the animals. Then Saul said, "Come on. Let's go back to my father. He may worry about us."

"Not yet," said Saul's servant. "Let's go on to the next city. A man of God lives there. Perhaps he can tell us where we should look for the donkeys." So they walked to the city.

When Samuel looked at Saul, the Lord spoke to him, saying, "Here is the man I told you about. He shall rule over My people."

Then Saul came near Samuel and asked, "Tell me, please, where does the man of God live?"

Samuel answered, "I am that man. Come with me to the place where I offer sacrifices. Eat with me today, and I will tell you the reason for your journey. As for your donkeys that were lost, they have been found."

Saul ate with Samuel and stayed overnight. The next day Saul was ready to go back home. Samuel walked with Saul and his servant to the edge of the city. Then he said, "Tell your servant to go on. I don't want him to hear what I'm going to tell you."

Samuel took a small bottle of oil and poured it on Saul's head. He kissed Saul and blessed him in the name of the Lord. Samuel told Saul of certain things he would see which would prove that he, Saul, had indeed been chosen by the Lord.

Samuel said, "Today you will meet two men, and they will say to you, 'The donkeys you're looking for are found. Now your father is worrying about you.' After that you will meet three men going to worship God. One of the men will be carrying three loaves of bread, another will have three goats, and the last man will be holding a skin-bottle. They will speak to you and give you two loaves of bread.

"After that," continued Samuel, "you will come to the hill of God. There you will meet some men praising God with the harp and flute. When you get to the town of Gilgal, stay there till I come to you."

Saul said good-bye to Samuel and went on his way. He saw all the things which Samuel had told him about.

After a week Samuel called all the people together. "You have said that you want a king. You want him to rule over you instead of God." Then Samuel called for Saul to stand in front of the people, and because he was so tall, he stood out above them all.

"This is the man," said Samuel, "whom the Lord has chosen to be king." And all the people shouted, "Long live the king!"

Then Samuel told the people what the king's duties would be. At first everyone was not ready to have Saul as king. Some people said, "We don't even know this young man. How do we know that he will be a good king?"

Before long an enemy king decided to fight God's people. Right away Saul sent word to everyone to come and get ready to fight. Saul and his men marched over the mountains to the land of the enemy. There the Lord helped Saul and his men win the battle. It was a great victory. After that everyone was glad to have Saul as king.

—1 Samuel 8—10:24

David, Second King of Israel

Saul had every chance to be a good king. But he was not! He wanted his own way. Saul did not want to run the country as God told him to do. Soon Saul thought he was the best and most important person alive. He did what he wanted to do and he lied about bad things he had done.

One day Samuel found Saul on a mountainside where Saul was about to set up a statue of himself. "Hello," Saul said, "here I am obeying the Lord."

"Stop!" said Samuel. "Last night the Lord told me how you have been disobeying Him. Don't lie about it! The Lord knows what you have done. Now He has told me that He is going to make someone else king."

Saul was terribly afraid. He had thought he could do whatever he wanted and the Lord would be with him. He did not want to believe what Samuel said.

One day the Lord told Samuel to go to Bethlehem, where he would find a new king. "Find a man called Jesse," the Lord told Samuel.

Samuel obeyed and went to Bethlehem, where he found Jesse and one of his eight sons. As soon as Samuel saw the tall young man, he thought, "Here is the new king." But God said to Samuel, "Look, you are noticing how tall and strong the young man is. I am looking into his mind. A man's thoughts are more important than how his body looks. This man is not the one to be the next king."

Jesse asked each of his sons to meet Samuel. Samuel looked carefully at each one. After he had looked at seven boys, he said, "Jesse, do you have any more sons?"

"Yes," said Jesse, "I have one more, but he is away taking care of the sheep."

"Send for him," said Samuel.

When David came and stood before Samuel, Samuel looked into the boy's eyes and seemed to be thinking. The Lord was telling Samuel to make this boy the king. Then Samuel took an animal horn he had brought with him. He poured some oil into it. "Jesse," he said, "this boy David will be a great king over our people. God will make him to be greater than Saul. Saul will be

king for a time, but some day David will be king because God has chosen him." Then Samuel poured the oil on David's head.

After that David went back to his sheep. He would wait till time for God to make him the king.

—1 Samuel 15:10-26; 16:1-13

David Meets an Enemy

Sometime after Samuel visited Jesse, there was a war and three of Jesse's older sons went off to fight. David stayed home to help with the sheep and the other work. One day Jesse said to David, "Take this basket of roasted corn and these ten loaves of bread to your brothers in the army. Give this cheese to their captain and see how your brothers are getting along."

So David left the sheep with another shepherd and started off for the battlefield. He got to the soldiers' camp just as the men were leaving to fight. Soon the enemy soldiers and King Saul's soldiers stood facing each other in two long lines.

Then a huge soldier stepped out from the enemy's line of men. He was a tall giant, and he shouted to King Saul's men. "Send me a man who will fight me," he yelled.

As soon as King Saul's men saw him, they ran away. But David was not afraid. He wanted to learn more about the giant Goliath.

Now, when David's oldest brother heard that David was asking questions about fighting the giant, he was angry. "What are you doing here anyway?" he asked.

"What have I done wrong?" David asked. And he asked some other soldiers about the giant. Finally, one soldier told King Saul about David, and the king sent for David to come to him.

"How can a boy like you," asked King Saul, "possibly fight a giant like Goliath?"

David then told the king that he had killed a lion and a bear to keep them from harming his father's sheep. "The Lord who helped me kill wild animals will also help me kill the giant," said David.

"All right," King Saul said after David had

proved that he could trust the Lord to help him. "Go ahead, boy. May the Lord be with you."

David picked up five smooth stones to use in his sling. He took his shepherd's staff and started off to meet Goliath.

Goliath was very angry when he saw a boy instead of a strong soldier coming to fight him. "What?" he yelled, "am I a dog that you send someone with a stick? Come here, boy. I'll kill you and give you to the birds and the wild animals to eat."

"You come to me," said David, "with a sword and sharp spear, but I come to you in the name of the Lord. Today the Lord will help me kill you, and the whole world will find out that God is great and powerful!"

As Goliath started for David, David ran to meet him. David reached into his bag and took out one of the stones. He put it in his sling and shot the stone at the giant. The stone hit Goliath very hard on his forehead. Goliath fell to the ground, and David grabbed his sword and killed him.

Then King Saul's men came running and chased the enemy soldiers. That day the Lord helped David and King Saul's men win the war.

—1 Samuel 17:1-53

A New Home for David

After David killed the giant, he lived at the palace with King Saul and Jonathan, Saul's son. When David met Jonathan the first time, the boys liked each other and became good friends.

Jonathan told David that he would like to make him his brother. He gave David his sword, belt, bow and arrows, and his special robe which showed that he was the son of a king.

King Saul gave David special work to do, and David did his work very well. The time came when Saul was so pleased with David's work that he made David commander of the army.

But soon Saul was sorry that he had made David commander. After a battle, when the soldiers came home, all of the people were shouting, "Saul has killed his thousands, but David has killed his ten thousands."

Of course Saul was angry. "They give David credit for killing ten thousands," Saul said to himself, "but they say I have not killed as many. If the people keep on liking David so much,

they'll make him king instead of me."

The more Saul thought about the people's cheering, the more angry and jealous he became. In fact, the very next day Saul tried to kill David. David was playing his harp, as he often did, to make the king happy. Suddenly, without any warning, Saul picked up a spear and threw it at David. God took care of David and caused him to jump to one side. The spear missed him.

Next the angry king told David to get out of the palace. He never wanted to see David again. Saul told both his son and his soldiers to find David and kill him.

Jonathan talked with his father and tried to get King Saul to promise that he would not hurt David. But the king would not make a promise and keep it. Jonathan felt terrible. He told David that

he would talk with his father one more time. "If I can't get him to promise to leave you alone," said Jonathan, "you will have to leave."

"How will I know how your father feels about me?" asked David. Jonathan told him about a secret signal.

King Saul was angry to have David around, but he was also angry when David wasn't in the palace. "Why hasn't David been here for dinner today or yesterday?" King Saul asked Jonathan. Jonathan made an excuse for David. This made Saul angrier than ever. "Go get him so I can kill him," Saul yelled at Jonathan.

"But what has he done?" Jonathan asked. Then Saul threw a spear at Jonathan, his own son. At last Jonathan saw that his father meant it when he said that David should be killed.

The next morning Jonathan went to the field where David was hiding. He took a bow and arrow with him, and one of his servants, a young boy.

"Start running," Jonathan told the boy. "I'll shoot the arrows and you can find them." The boy started off, and Jonathan shot an arrow. "The arrow is far beyond you," called Jonathan. "Hurry. Get it." The boy got the arrow and brought it back. He did not know that Jonathan's words had been a signal to David. The words told David he would have to leave right away.

Jonathan told the boy to take his bow and arrows back to the palace. Then David crawled out from the bushes where he had been hiding. The two young men promised to be friends forever. Then Jonathan went back to the palace and David ran off to hide from the king.

For the rest of his life, King Saul tried to catch David and kill him. But he never could. God was taking care of David.

Once again there was war. King Saul, Jonathan, and all the soldiers fought. Jonathan was killed. And when King Saul saw that his men were losing, he used his own sword to kill himself. David heard about it and felt very sad. He had lost his good friend Jonathan.

—1 Samuel 18:1-14; 20:12-42; 31:1-4, 6

Jeremiah, God's Prophet

King David was a great and good king. And the next king, David's son Solomon, was a very wise king. But Solomon was not the good king his father had been. Solomon did not love the Lord and obey Him as his father had done.

One day God told Solomon that because Solomon had not obeyed Him, his son could not be king over all the Jews. The Lord said that Solomon's son could have part of the kingdom. All of the people were divided into 12 tribes. Solomon's son was to be king over two tribes. Another man would be king over the other 10 tribes.

The Bible tells of the 19 men who had their turn at being king of the 10 tribes. Most of these men forgot to worship God. They did more than forget; they said they would not worship God. Instead, they worshiped idols.

Some of the men who had a turn at being king over the two tribes were good. But some of them were also bad kings.

God was very patient. Through all the years He kept sending special men to tell about Him. Some of these men were called prophets. Their work was to tell the people about God and also tell about the things that God was going to cause to happen. One prophet who had a very difficult job was Jeremiah.

Jeremiah was born when a good king was in charge of the two tribes. The good king was King Josiah. Josiah had become king when he was only eight years old. When Josiah was about 16, he let people know that he was going to love and obey the Lord God. He soon began to throw out the idols. He was careful to destroy every temple where idols had been worshiped. King Josiah saw to it that the altars built to worship idols were broken down. He burned the idols themselves.

King Josiah had done his part to get the people ready to think about God. Jeremiah was the man God wanted to speak to the people. God told Jeremiah exactly what he was to do. The Lord said, "I have appointed you, Jeremiah, to speak for Me."

"Oh," said Jeremiah, "I can't do that."

But God would not let Jeremiah say no. God said, "Don't say you won't speak for Me, for you will go wherever I send you and speak whatever I tell you to say. Don't be afraid of the people, for I am with you."

Then the Lord gave Jeremiah a vision or dream. He asked Jeremiah what he saw, and Jeremiah said, "I see a pot of boiling water. It is tipping, and some of the water is spilling out."

"That pot," said the Lord, "is a picture of what is going to happen to the Jews. An enemy will come and spill over the people of this land.

This is the way I will punish My people for forgetting Me and for worshiping idols. Now, Jeremiah, you will soon tell My people what is going to happen."

King Josiah, the king at the time Jeremiah had his dream, ordered all Jews to come to Jerusalem to worship God. The king also asked Jeremiah to talk to the people about God. The people obeyed and came to Jerusalem, but they did not come because they wanted to worship God. They came to obey the king, as they knew they must do.

Then Jeremiah talked to the people. He told them how many years before, God had brought His people out of Egypt with Moses as their leader. Jeremiah asked the people to remember all the good things God had done for them. Then Jeremiah told the people that they had not obeyed God. They had not thanked Him for what He had done. They had not even been thinking about Him. Jeremiah called them wicked, selfish, and greedy. He said that if the people did not change their ways and ask God to forgive them, God would punish them.

The people were angry with Jeremiah when he told them the truth. They said, "Let's kill him." But God took care of his prophet, and the people did not kill him.

About this time, the king of Egypt came with some of his soldiers. He said that he had not come to fight, but King Josiah did not believe Him. King Josiah made war with the king of Egypt, and in the fight Josiah was killed.

A new king came to the throne, and God told Jeremiah to tell this king what was going to happen. This time Jeremiah spoke to the king's officers and other men in government jobs. He said, "Look, you have the Temple here at Jerusalem, but no one really worships God. Poor people are suffering, and no one cares. God asks you to change your ways." But the government men would not listen either.

Then God commanded Jeremiah to write in a scroll all of the punishments that would come because people disobeyed Him. Jeremiah asked Baruch, a man trained in writing, to put down his message.

Baruch took the scroll and read the message to the king and his officers. The king was sitting near a fire because it was winter and he wanted to keep warm. After the king had heard part of the message, he took a knife and cut that part of the scroll. Then he threw the message in the fire. When the next part of the scroll was read to him, he did the same thing. The king burned the whole scroll. He would not listen, and he was very angry with Jeremiah and Baruch for

giving God's message. In fact, if he could have found them, the king would have killed both Jeremiah and Baruch. But the two men were hiding, and God was keeping them safe.

The people hated Jeremiah for telling them about their wrongdoing. Jeremiah told the Lord about it. He said, "Lord, I have not hurt any of the people, but they are angry with me. They all say bad things about me." The Lord again told Jeremiah that He would take care of him. He also said that when the enemy came to take Jerusalem, Jeremiah would be kept safe.

One day the Lord said to Jeremiah, "Buy a clay jar and take it to the east gate of the city. Take some of the officials with you and some of the older priests from the Temple. Speak to them the words that I give you."

Jeremiah obeyed. When he stood near the east gate with some of the men, he spoke the words God told him to say. "Listen to the word of the Lord," said Jeremiah. "Citizens of Jerusalem, the Lord God says that He will bring terrible evil on this place. You have turned away from God. The people burn incense to idols. But some day the Lord will let enemy armies come in and kill you. God says, 'I will wipe Jerusalem off the Earth.' "

Then the Lord told Jeremiah to throw the jar against the wall. "This is the message from the Lord," said Jeremiah as he smashed the jar. "As this jar lies smashed, so the Lord will smash the people of Jerusalem. As this jar cannot be mended, neither can the people expect to put Jerusalem together. The city and the people will be destroyed."

Jerusalem is captured

The time for God to punish His people was coming nearer. Jeremiah gave them God's message, but the people still would not listen. They did not believe that God would let an enemy people capture them.

One day the Jews heard that King Nebuchadnezzar of Babylon was coming to fight. When King Nebuchadnezzar captured Jerusalem, he took many of the Jews with him. Then King Nebuchadnezzar told Zedekiah to be in charge of the people who were left in Jerusalem. He also made Zedekiah promise to obey him.

After the Jews who went with King Nebuchadnezzar reached Babylon, Jeremiah wrote them a letter. He told them to try to be content, to worship God, and to remember that someday, if they asked God to forgive them, God would let them come back to Jerusalem. Jeremiah stayed in Jerusalem and kept on telling the people to turn from their wicked ways. "Ask God's forgiveness," he said, "and worship Him."

Now, Zedekiah did not do his work well. He himself was against King Nebuchadnezzar. He let the people do as they wanted. And Zedekiah was very angry with Jeremiah for all that he had said. He had Jeremiah put into prison.

Zedekiah said, "Whose side are you on, Jeremiah? You live here in Jerusalem. You are a Jew, but you tell me that the King of Babylon is going to come and fight us. In fact, you say that the Lord God is going to help King Nebuchadnezzar win." So Jeremiah was put in prison for telling the truth. Jeremiah's prison was a deep well. The men had to use ropes to lower him into it.

King Zedekiah was afraid of Jeremiah. He did not want him to live, but he did not want him to die either. So when some of this men told him that Jeremiah might die down in the well, he told them to bring him up. The king took Jeremiah out of the well, but he did not let him go. He asked Jeremiah to come and talk with him.

"Now tell me the truth this time, Jeremiah," said wicked King Zedekiah.

"If I tell you the truth, will you have me killed?" asked Jeremiah. The king promised that he would not kill Jeremiah. Then he asked the prophet what he should do. Zedekiah said, "If I surrender to King Nebuchadnezzar, I am afraid that he will give me to my own soldiers. They would be so very angry with me if I gave myself up that they might kill me."

"No," said Jeremiah, "King Nebuchadnezzar will not do that. Obey the Lord and all will be well. But if you don't give yourself up to King Nebuchadnezzar, he will keep fighting till you do. You and all your family will be killed."

But King Zedekiah was angry to hear God's message. He had Jeremiah put in another prison. And he kept on fighting for more than a year. It was a terrible war!

One night King Zedekiah and part of his army tried to escape from the city. But they were caught. Then King Nebuchadnezzar killed Zedekiah's sons. He had Zedekiah's eyes poked out. Blind Zedekiah was bound with chains and kept in a prison in Babylon till he died.

King Nebuchadnezzar ordered his army to burn the city of Jerusalem and the Temple. The army also broke down the big wall that was around the city. And King Nebuchadnezzar also took many more Jews away. He left only a few people to work in the fields.

During the fighting between Zedekiah and King Nebuchadnezzar, Jeremiah was in prison. The Lord came to Jeremiah to comfort him. He said to Jeremiah, "Call to Me, and I will answer you, and show you great and mighty things, which you cannot even imagine." Jeremiah talked with the Lord, and the Lord showed him how He was going to take care of His people. "Someday," the Lord told Jeremiah, "My people will live in Jerusalem again. In that day everything will be right and fair and honest."

King Nebuchadnezzar had planned to take Jeremiah to Babylon too. But it happened that one of the captains in the king's army knew Jeremiah. When he saw the prophet in chains and waiting to go to Babylon, the captain took the chains off Jeremiah. The captain said, "Jeremiah, you can choose whether you want to stay here or go to Babylon." God was using the captain to keep Jeremiah safe as He had promised.

Jeremiah decided to stay in the land with the Jews who were left behind. Nebuchadnezzar made Gedaliah, a Jew, governor of the land. He could not live in the city of Jerusalem because Nebuchadnezzar had burned it to the ground. But Gedaliah had a good place to live.

Now, when the fighting between Zedekiah and Nebuchadnezzar first started, some Jews had run away. They had been hiding in other lands. When they heard that Gedaliah was now governor, they wanted to come back to their homeland. Gedaliah told them to came back, to work hard, and to serve the king of Babylon. Most of the men did just that. But one man hated Gedaliah. He came to the governor's house for dinner. Then, when he had a chance, he killed Gedaliah, the governor.

When the other Jews who had come back heard this bad news, they were afraid. They thought that King Nebuchadnezzar would blame them for Gedaliah's death and have them killed. The men asked Jeremiah what to do, and he said he would ask the Lord.

After Jeremiah had prayed for 10 days, he called the men together. "The Lord has told me that if you will stay here in the land, the Lord will take care of you. The king of Babylon will not hurt you. But if you run away to Egypt, as you are thinking of doing, you will be killed in Egypt. You will never see your own land again."

The men talked it over. They decided that they would not trust the Lord to keep them. They went to Egypt, taking Jeremiah with them. And the men were killed in Egypt, just as the Lord had told Jeremiah. But the Lord kept Jeremiah safe. And Jeremiah lived in the land of Egypt till it was time for him to die.

—*Jeremiah*

Ezekiel Has a Dream

God's people, called the Israelites or Jews, were no longer free. They had been taken prisoners by an enemy country. God had warned His people that this would happen if they kept on disobeying Him. For hundreds of years, God had been telling them that He would protect the people if they loved Him and obeyed Him. But the people disobeyed. They prayed to God when they were in trouble, but the rest of the time they did as they pleased. Finally the time came for God to punish His disobedient people. He let an enemy capture them.

But God also gave His people another chance to hear His Word. Among the people taken captive was Ezekiel, a man who loved God and tried to get other people to love Him too. God gave Ezekiel dreams or visions, and He helped Ezekiel understand the dreams.

One dream that the Lord gave Ezekiel was about some old bones. Ezekiel seemed to be in a valley. And all about him were bones—bones from the skeletons of men who had died.

"Son of man," said the Lord God to Ezekiel, "look at these bones. Is there any life here? Can these bones live again?"

Ezekiel said, "Lord, You know. I don't."

Then the Lord God told Ezekiel to talk to the bones. God told Ezekiel what to say, and Ezekiel obeyed.

"Oh, dry bones," said Ezekiel, "listen to the Word of the Lord. The Lord says He will cause you to live again. He will put breath into you. He will put muscle and flesh and skin over you. You will live and know that He is God."

Then in his dream, Ezekiel heard a noise. It was the sound of bones shaking and moving as they

came together to form skeletons. The bones and skin became bodies, but they were not yet living people.

God told Ezekiel what to say next. "Come from the four winds, O Spirit," said Ezekiel as he obeyed God. "Spirit, breathe on these bodies that they may live again."

Then God sent breath to the bodies, and they lived. As the men stood up, they made up a very great army. As Ezekiel looked at the men, God told him what the dream was about.

"Ezekiel, I am showing you a picture of My people. My people are like the bones. They think that their nation is dead because they are in an enemy land. But they will not be in the enemy land forever. Someday I will send them back to live in their own land. When the bones came back to life, I was showing you how My people will feel when they know that they can go back to their own land.

"Someday My people will love Me, and I will be their God. Tell My people about your dream. When My people know what is going to happen, they will feel better about living in an enemy land. They will know that good things will come to them."

And Ezekiel told the people his dream.

—*Ezekiel 37*

Three Brave Men

After King Nebuchadnezzar had captured Jerusalem, he took many of the strongest and smartest Jews to Babylon. The Jews were in Babylon for many years. Those years are called the time of the Exile.

Many of the people who were exiled forgot about God. But many of them remembered Him and kept on worshiping Him. It was not easy to worship God in a strange land where most people, including the king, worshiped idols. And sometimes the king made it hard for people to worship the Lord God. How could a king make it hard to worship God? This story tells of one way King Nebuchadnezzar made it hard for people to show their love and trust in God.

The morning sun shone brightly on a high golden statue that had been set up the day before. The golden statue was as tall as a building eight or ten floors high. The golden statue could be seen for miles. And that was exactly what King Nebuchadnezzar wanted.

The statue was of King Nebuchadnezzar. Clever workmen had made it. Now it was time for the special service when everyone would bow down and worship the statue.

All of the people had obeyed the king's order to come to the Plain of Dura in the land of Babylon. Now they waited before the statue of gold to see what would happen next.

A trumpet sounded and the king's messenger walked out to stand before the people, ready to read the king's message. He read, "To you it is commanded, O people, that when you hear the band begin to play, fall down and worship King Nebuchadnezzar's golden statue. If anyone does not obey the king's command, he shall be thrown into a fiery, flaming furnace."

Then King Nebuchadnezzar told the band to begin to play, and everyone bowed low before the statue. Everyone, that is, except three men. These men, named Shadrach, Meshach, and Abednego, worshiped the Lord God. They would not bow down and worship a statue of the king.

Some of the king's men decided to watch the three men. They wanted to be sure that Shadrach, Meshach, and Abednego were not worshiping the king's statue. Then they planned to report the three men to the king. Perhaps they expected to get a reward.

It was not very many days before the band played again. The music filled the air, and all the people fell upon the ground and worshiped. The king's officers looked around. They could not see Meshach, Shadrach, and Abednego anywhere. The three men had stayed at home and prayed.

The officers hurried off to the king's palace. "O King," they said when King Nebuchadnezzar told them to speak, "we want to ask about the rule you made. Did you not say, O King, that everyone should worship your statue? Did you not say that anyone who refused to worship should be thrown into a flaming furnace?"

"Yes," said King Nebuchadnezzar, "I made that rule. I said that the fiery, flaming furnace would be the punishment. Now what?"

"Well," said the officers, "we know three men —Shadrach, Meshach, and Abednego—who are not paying any attention to your rule. They do not bow down when the band begins to play."

Then the king sent for the three men. He asked, "Is it true, Shadrach, Meshach, and Abednego, that you do not bow down and worship my statue?"

"Yes," said the three men, "it is true. We worship only our great Lord God. We cannot worship your statue. Even if you throw us into the flaming fiery furnace, we cannot change. We must obey our God. Our God is able to keep us even in the flaming furnace. But if He lets us burn, then that is all right, too. Please know, O King, that we will never serve your gods or worship your statue."

After this brave speech, the king was very angry. His face got red, and he commanded that the furnace be made seven times hotter than ever before. Then he called for some of the strongest men in his army to tie up Shadrach, Meshach, and Abednego.

The soldiers bound the three men with ropes and threw them into the furnace. And because the king had ordered the fire to be hotter than ever before, the flames killed the soldiers when they got close to the furnace.

Shadrach, Meshach, and Abednego fell into the flames of the fiery furnace. King Nebuchadnezzar expected them to be burned up right away. But when he looked, he saw four men standing in the furnace.

"Look," he screamed, "I see four men walking around in the flames. How can this be? The fourth man looks like the Son of God!"

Then King Nebuchadnezzar came to the open door of the furnace. He called, "Shadrach, Meshach, and Abednego, servants of the Most High God, come out!"

And the three men stepped out of the fire. Everyone could see that their clothes had not been touched by the flames. Neither the men's hair nor their skin was burned.

Then Nebuchadnezzar said, "Blessed be the God of Shadrach, Meshach, and Abednego. He took care of His servants when they were willing to die rather than disobey Him. Now I shall make a new law. No one must say anything against the God that these three men worship. He alone is God. If any man does talk against God, that man shall have his house knocked down and he himself will be killed."

Then the king gave the three men better jobs.
—*Daniel 3*

68

Daniel Tells God's Message

King Nebuchadnezzar had been dead for five years. King Belshazzar was the new ruler. And he did not want to have anything to do with the Lord God, whom King Nebuchadnezzar had come to worship.

One night King Belshazzar gave a very important dinner party. He invited one thousand people to come to the party. He decided to serve wine in some special cups which had been in the beautiful Temple at Jerusalem. The cups had been used in the Temple, but now Belshazzar was going to use them to drink to idols.

Suddenly, as the guests were drinking from the special cups, they saw the fingers of a man's hand writing on the palace wall. The king was terribly afraid.

"Bring some magicians," King Belshazzar screamed. "Bring someone who can tell me what that writing says. Whoever reads that writing will be dressed in royal clothing. And he shall be the third ruler in the kingdom."

Magicians were brought to the king. They looked at the writing on the wall, but not one of them could tell the king the words.

The king became more and more afraid. Now his soldiers and officers began to be afraid too.

Then someone thought of sending for Daniel. Someone remembered what a help Daniel had been to King Nebuchadnezzar. Daniel was a friend to Meshach, Shadrach, and Abednego. Daniel, too, worshiped the Lord God.

When Daniel stood before King Belshazzar, he let the king know that God would help him give the meaning of the writing. Daniel also told the king that he should have been worshiping God. "Your father, King Nebuchadnezzar, worshiped God," said Daniel. "You should have been worshiping the Lord God yourself. But you have been against Him. You have even taken the special cups from His Temple to use in drinking to your idols. God caused the writing to appear on the wall. This is His message: God is finished with you. You have not believed in God. Now He is going to take your kingdom from you."

Daniel had told what the writing meant. The king kept his word and had special clothing brought for Daniel. And he was made the third ruler in the kingdom.

God kept His word. That very night King Belshazzar was killed. And the kingdom was taken over by his enemies.

—Daniel 5

Daniel Dares to Pray

Belshazzar, the king of Babylon, was dead. Darius took over the kingdom. And Darius chose 120 governors to be in charge of different parts of the country. Then Darius told the governors that they were to report to three men. Darius called the three men presidents. One of the three presidents was Daniel. This Daniel was the same one who had told King Belshazzar the meaning of the writing that suddenly appeared on the wall of the palace.

Now, Daniel did such good work for King Darius that the king was thinking of making him the second ruler in the kingdom. Then Daniel would be almost as important as the king himself. Of course, the other presidents and the 120 governors were very unhappy. They did not want to see Daniel almost as important as the king himself. So they looked around to see what Daniel might be doing that was wrong. If they could find Daniel doing wrong, they would tell the king. Then the king might change his mind about Daniel.

The governors and other chief officers watched and watched. But they could not find anything wrong with Daniel.

One day some of the men had an idea and rushed off to tell the king. "O King Darius," they began, "all of us who are your officers have agreed that you should make a new law. We would like you to say that for a month no one may ask anything of anyone except you. If anyone is found praying to a god or an idol, that person shall be punished by being thrown into a den of lions. O King, make this law and sign it, so that even you cannot change it."

The king listened to the men and decided that their idea was a good one. And King Darius signed the new law.

When Daniel heard that the new law had been made, he did not stop praying to God. Three times a day Daniel opened his window, knelt at the window, and prayed to God. In the morning, Daniel prayed. At noon he would leave his work, go home, and kneel to pray. Then he would go back to work. At the end of the day Daniel would go home and, before he went to bed, he would pray again.

Of course, the men who were watching Daniel soon found out that he was still praying to the Lord God. The men knew that Daniel was not keeping the king's new law. And they were glad that Daniel was breaking the law. They hurried

off to tell the king what Daniel was doing.

"King Darius, live forever," they said as they bowed before the king on his throne. "Didn't you sign your name to the law that for a month no one can ask anything of anyone but you? Doesn't the new law say that anyone who breaks it shall be thrown into a den of lions?"

"Yes," said King Darius, "I made that law."

The men were pleased. "Well, King," they said, "Daniel is breaking the law. He must be thrown into a den of lions."

Poor King Darius. He had forgotten that Daniel prayed to the Lord God. Now Daniel would have to be thrown into a den of lions. The king studied the law all day, trying to find a way to keep Daniel out of the lions' den. But the king could not find any way to help Daniel.

At sunset the king had to give in and call his soldiers. He had to tell them to take Daniel and throw him into the den of lions.

The men took Daniel and threw him into the lions' den. The king was there, and he called to Daniel, "O Daniel, I hope your God can save you in some way." Then the king went home. He was miserable! Poor King Darius! He could not eat nor sleep. He kept thinking about Daniel.

Early in the morning the king hurried back to the lions' den. King Darius called to Daniel, "Daniel, Daniel, was your God able to keep you safe?"

The king waited. Then he heard a voice. "Your Majesty, live forever," Daniel called. "My God has taken care of me. He sent an angel to close the lions' mouth so that they could not hurt me. God knows that when I pray to Him I am not hurting you."

Then the king ordered that Daniel be taken from the lions' den. And not a scratch was found on Daniel. God had kept him perfectly safe.

The king punished the men who had tried to hurt Daniel. And then he wrote a letter to all nations. The king's letter said, "Peace to all people on the Earth. I make a new law that everyone should honor Daniel's God. He is the true and living God. He takes care of His own. He does wonders both on the Earth and in heaven. He kept Daniel safe from the lions. And after that, Daniel got along very well with King Darius.

—Daniel 6

Zerubbabel and His Work

God had told His people that they would have to stay in Babylon for 70 years. Now His words were coming true. It was time for the people to go back to their own land.

King Cyrus of Babylon wrote a letter. His letter said, "The Lord God has told me to help rebuild His Temple in Jerusalem. All of God's people who are now living in Babylon may go back to Jerusalem."

King Cyrus also commanded that the gold and silver that had been taken from Jerusalem should be sent back. The king did his very best to help God's people get back to their own land. He chose a priest by the name of Zerubbabel to be in charge of everything.

God took care of His people so that they were kept safe on the long trip from Babylon to Jerusalem. No one was robbed or killed.

When the people got to Jerusalem, they found that the city walls and the Temple had been torn down. The people fixed up the altar where sacrifices were made to the Lord. The people used the altar everyday to make sacrifices to the Lord and to worship Him. The people wanted God to help them.

God did give the people His help. Soon they had built up Jerusalem, the city walls, and the Temple. Then the people had a special time of giving thanks to the Lord.

—*Ezra 1—3*

Jonah, the Prophet, Decides to Obey

"Get up, Jonah!" said the Lord God to a man who lived near Nazareth. "Go to Nineveh. Tell them that the Lord is going to destroy them because they are so wicked."

Nineveh! Jonah did not want to go there. It was 600 miles from his home. That was a long way to walk or travel by donkey. Then, too, the people who lived in Nineveh were the most powerful people in the world at that time.

Jonah heard the Lord's message, but did he get up and obey? No. Instead he said to himself, "Nineveh! The people of Nineveh are strong and cruel and wicked. I have heard what they have done to their enemies. They ought to be punished. Someday they may come here and conquer my people."

Jonah did not want to take God's message to Nineveh. He thought he could run away from God, and so he went down to the harbor to find a ship on which he could travel. There was a ship ready to sail across the sea to Tarshish. Jonah bought a ticket and went on board. Jonah did not stay on deck, but went down into the ship. There he thought he could hide from the Lord God.

Soon the ship set sail, but suddenly a terrible storm came up. The Lord had sent a strong wind and rain. The sailors were afraid that the ship would sink. They cried to their gods to protect them. Then they began to unload some of the cargo. The sailors thought that by throwing some of the cargo overboard they would lighten the ship. Then the ship would be able to ride out the storm. But nothing seemed to help. The ship tossed and rolled till it seemed that it would be broken in pieces.

The captain of the ship asked everyone on board to pray to his god. When the captain heard that Jonah was asleep below deck, he went to him.

"Hey, you, get up!" the captain yelled at Jonah. "How do you dare sleep in this storm? Start praying to your god, and perhaps your god will save us."

The storm got worse, and the sailors became more frightened. One of them said, "This storm has been sent by the gods. They must be angry with someone on board. Who is it?"

The sailors decided to find out who had made the gods angry. They said, "Let's draw straws to find out which man has displeased the gods. The man who gets the shortest straw is the one to blame."

Every man on board ship took a straw. When everyone had his straw, they looked to see who had the shortest one. And Jonah had it.

"Who are you?" the sailors asked Jonah. "What have you done? Has your God sent this storm because of what you have done?"

Jonah told them that he was a Jew. He also said, "I worship the God of Heaven, who made the Earth and sea. But right now I am running away from Him."

"Why did you do that?" asked the frightened men. Then they asked, "What shall we do to you, so that the storm will stop?"

Jonah told them to throw him overboard. He said, "I know this terrible storm has come because of me. Pick me up and throw me into the sea. Then the sea will quiet down."

The sailors did not want to throw Jonah overboard. They took oars and tried to guide the ship to shore, but they could not. They prayed to God. "We beg You, Lord," they prayed, "do not blame us for throwing this man overboard." Then they picked up Jonah and threw him into the sea. As soon as Jonah hit the water, the storm stopped. The sailors were amazed! They knelt down and prayed to God.

Now, God had planned for a huge fish to swallow Jonah. And as soon as Jonah was in the water, the fish came along and swallowed him in one gulp. Jonah was inside the huge fish for three days and nights.

While Jonah was inside the fish, he had time to think and pray. Here are some of the words

Jonah in his prayer to God:

"Oh, Lord, in my great trouble I prayed to You, and You heard me. You listened to my voice.

"You threw me into the sea. I sank into the water and was covered by Your wild and stormy waves. The waters closed above me. The plants in the water wrapped themselves about my head. I thought I would never see Your Temple again.

"But, Lord, you have snatched me from death. You have kept me.

"Lord, I will worship You. I will make sacrifices to You. I promise that I will worship You alone."

The Lord listened to Jonah's prayer. He knew Jonah felt sorry for what he had done. And the Lord ordered the fish to spit Jonah up on the land. How thankful Jonah was when he found himself safe on dry land.

The Lord spoke to Jonah again, saying, "Jonah, I am asking you to go to Nineveh, that wicked city. There you are to preach about Me. I will tell you what you are to say."

This time Jonah obeyed. He set off for Nineveh right away. After he reached Nineveh, Jonah walked from the edge of the city toward the center for a whole day. As he walked, he preached, saying "Forty days from now God will destroy wicked Nineveh!" Over and over Jonah repeated his message. Crowds gathered about him. The people were afraid. They knew that they were wicked. They knew that they deserved to be punished. They believed Jonah. And they cried out to God to forgive them.

Everyone, including the king, felt sorry. The people put on sackcloth—cloth that was coarse like burlap—to show how sorry they were. The king put aside his beautiful robes and put on sackcloth too.

The king wanted to be sure that everyone was asking God's forgiveness. He sent word by special messengers that everyone should pray to God. He said, "Let no one, not even the animals, eat anything or drink anything — not even water. Everyone must dress in sackcloth and pray to God. Let every person turn from his wicked ways. Who can tell? Perhaps even yet God will decide to let us live."

And when the Lord God saw how sorry the people felt, He did not destroy them. God forgave them for their wrongdoing. And the people were very glad.

This news should have made Jonah happy. The people had listened to his message and believed him. But Jonah was not happy. In fact, he was angry because God had forgiven the people. Jonah said to God, "Lord, this is just what I thought You would do. I did not want to come here in the first place. You know, Lord, that the people of Nineveh and all the other Assyrians are enemies of the Jews. We are afraid of them. We would be glad to see something happen to them. But now You are being as good to them as You are to us. You really are being a Friend to our enemies."

The Lord said, "Jonah, is it right for you to be

angry like this? If the people are sorry for their sin, shouldn't I forgive them?"

But Jonah would not answer the Lord. He went out to the edge of the city and pouted. Jonah sat and waited to see what would happen to the city.

The powerful Lord God knew how Jonah felt. The same God who had sent the storm at sea and the great fish to swallow Jonah now caused a vine to grow. The vine grew up overnight. Its large leaves gave Jonah shade. Jonah was glad for the vine. He could keep cool as he waited to see what was going to happen to the wicked city of Nineveh.

But God was using this vine to teach Jonah a lesson. As Jonah sat under the vine, God sent a worm to attack the root of the vine so that it died. Then Jonah felt the hot sun.

Then God spoke to Jonah again. "Look, Jonah," He said, "why are you angry? You were glad for the vine. Now you are sorry that it has died because you cannot enjoy its shade anymore. It is strange you have such strong feelings about a vine, but no feelings about people. In Nineveh are thousands and thousands of people who did not know about Me till you came and told them. Are you angry because I have given them a chance to worship Me?"

—*Jonah 1—4*